I0803784

Discovering New Jersey's PINE BARRENS

Discovering New Jersey's
PINE BARRENS

Cathy Antener

The History Press

Published by The History Press
Charleston, SC 29403
www.historypress.net

Copyright © 2012 by Cathy Antener
All rights reserved

Unless otherwise noted, all images are by the author.

First published 2012

Manufactured in the United States

ISBN 978.1.60949.557.2

Library of Congress CIP data applied for.

Notice: The information in this book is true and complete to the best of our knowledge. It is offered without guarantee on the part of the author or The History Press. The author and The History Press disclaim all liability in connection with the use of this book.

All rights reserved. No part of this book may be reproduced or transmitted in any form whatsoever without prior written permission from the publisher except in the case of brief quotations embodied in critical articles and reviews.

Contents

Preface

For many people, the phrase "New Jersey Pine Barrens" conjures up images of dark, desolate forests of distorted pines, bloodcurdling screams in the night and piercing red eyes of what could be the Jersey Devil peeking out from behind a tree. While that just *might* be true, there are over a million acres in southern New Jersey filled with fascinating people, places and things man-made and natural—and perhaps a bit supernatural—waiting to be discovered by visitors to this mysterious and fascinating region that's just a short drive from Atlantic City, New York City and Philadelphia.

There is so much more to the Pine Barrens than its sweetly scented pine forests filled with blueberries, cranberries and endangered orchids. The hamlets, villages and towns in and around the area offer a plethora of attractions for visitors and residents alike. This is *not* the New Jersey you see when landing at Newark Liberty Airport, emerging from one of the tunnels out of New York City or from the lights and glamour of the Atlantic City casinos. The Pine Barrens is special, and its residents live differently than in the busy urban areas of New Jersey. As you read this book, you'll discover some of the towns that are the "gateways" to the Pine Barrens, as well as a few hamlets tucked deep within the protected preservation area. You'll read about the parks, museums, music, sports and where to go to explore the Pine Barrens without fear of getting lost in its million-plus acres and hundreds of miles of sugar-sand roads—or, perhaps most importantly, without running into the dreaded Jersey Devil!

The inhabitants of the Pine Barrens today are as interesting and varied as any region of the country. Some still live off the land, some own large farms, some are artists and others are doctors or lawyers. Some are sixth- or seventh-generation inhabitants; some proudly claim Lenni-Lenape heritage; others have only lived here a few years or less. Yet most have a common thread: a love of the Pines and everything it symbolizes. They will defend and protect the land, its plants, its animals and its people. Different people have different sources of pride, and that pride is apparent once you venture into the Pine Barrens and discover its magic.

This book should also help you to understand why conservationists want to protect the region from overpopulation. Once you have driven on a road deep in the Pines or along its bays, far away from the crowded cities, it should become clear how very special this area is to those who love it. Once you've stopped at a local restaurant or pub, it should also become clear how very special the people here are; they are clinging to a lifestyle and land on the precipice of disappearance. Hopefully, you, too, will come to love these forests, hamlets, wetlands and farms. When that happens, the Pinelands will get into your blood, and you will understand why we need to take care of this special area. Hopefully, you will want to help.

Discovering New Jersey's Pine Barrens is *not* filled with lot of scientific, environmental or historical information. There are dozens of excellent books written about the Pine Barrens: history, biology, mythology, boating, archaeology and agriculture—yes, the New Jersey Pine Barrens is actually agriculturally rich, despite its name. This book does include a bit of historic, nature-oriented and other significant information, but you won't find pages of technical data geared more toward scientists, historians, students or teachers. The purpose of this book is to introduce you to a Pine Barrens *you* can experience, whether you're traveling solo, with family and friends or just curled up in your armchair. Roughly divided into three regions—north, central and south—you'll find this book will provide you with an easy way to navigate this magical area and perhaps even help you to solve some of the mysteries associated with it. It by no means covers every special place in the Pines but should give you a good introduction to some of its delightful offerings.

If you're planning a trip to the East Coast of the United States, perhaps to Atlantic City, Wildwood or Long Beach Island, New Jersey; Philadelphia, Pennsylvania; New York City; or Washington, D.C., or even if you're just a local looking for a day of adventure, you'll find this book an invaluable guide to the charm, mystery and magic found in the New Jersey Pine Barrens, loaded with helpful travel tips to help make your stay fun and exciting. Just beware of the Jersey Devil!

Part I

Introduction to the New Jersey Pinelands

In order to understand New Jersey's Pine Barrens, also commonly referred to as "Pinelands," it's a good idea to become familiar with why these million-plus acres of forest are here, located between the two major metropolitan areas of Philadelphia and New York City, in one of the most populated areas of the United States. Once you realize the significance of its makeup, early industry, ecological importance and current measures being taken to protect the flora, fauna, history and culture, it will make visiting the many locations throughout this book much more memorable.

CHAPTER 1

Overview of the New Jersey Pinelands Region

The New Jersey Pinelands is a surprisingly diversified area of an otherwise populous state, from its sandy beaches to the dense pine oak forests where not a human sound can be heard. Of course, with its rich history, each journey into the Pines can be a new and exciting surprise. As odd as it may seem, this mysterious region is made up of more than one million acres nestled between Philadelphia and New York City, located in the fourth-smallest state in the country by area and second only to Washington, D.C., in population density. But before you venture out to the Pines, you really should know a bit about the Pinelands and how and why it's here.

PINELANDS V. PINE BARRENS

So what's the difference between "Pine Barrens" and "Pinelands"? This is a common question with a fairly straightforward explanation. The term "Pine Barrens" is commonly used to describe the ecological makeup of a region. The soil is sandy and acidic, which is a perfect environment for the pines, oaks, hollies, cranberries, blueberries and dozens of other plants that thrive in this terrain. Though New Jersey's is probably the best known, pine barrens terrains are located throughout the United States, in Long Island, New York, Wisconsin, North and South Carolina, Texas, Maine, Florida and several other states, as well as Canada. The traditional crops that European settlers brought with them to the colonies didn't thrive

A typical sugar-sand road in the New Jersey Pinelands. Roads such as these twist and turn throughout the forested areas. While they are usually hard-packed, the roads' edges are usually soft sand, and roads often become rutted, resulting in deep mud holes after a rain.

here; thus, the term "barrens" was coined. Of course, Native Americans knew that this land was not really barren at all and, over time, taught the settlers about those delicious red and blue gems we now call cranberries and blueberries. It's ironic that two of the three fruits indigenous to North America grow abundantly in a land once considered "barren" and are now reported to be so very beneficial to our health. The term "Pinelands" is actually a political demarcation, so delineated by both federal and state agencies, but both terms are used to describe the region in southern New Jersey that so many love, respect and protect.

The Pinelands is not all forest. Fifty-three municipalities within seven counties, having a total population of over 700,000, make up this fascinating region. Most of that population lives within either the "Regional Growth Area" or in one of several "Pinelands Towns," where you'll also find shops, restaurants, hotels and other essentials that you'll read about later in this book. "Pinelands Villages" are located within the Reserve, but building is restricted here, so little else other than a few shops will be found in many of these scenic locales. There are few major roads that traverse the Pine Barrens; the locals know shortcuts using sugar-sand roads, but it's not advisable to try these roads on your own, regardless of what electronic routing software might suggest.

Preservation

In 1967, a book entitled *The Pine Barrens* was written by John McPhee. This book brought to light the historical, cultural and ecological importance of the region, but more importantly, it also started a revolution of sorts; a few years earlier, the Pinelands Regional Planning Board had proposed a supersonic jetport to be located in southern Ocean and Burlington Counties. This jetport was to be the home of the Concorde jet and was going to be flanked by a planned city of 250,000 people. The approximate location was south of Route 72 in the twelve-thousand-acre Pygmy Forest (which is an

Bill Wasovich gives a tour of his home and property to well-known and respected birder Fred Lesser. Bill's home is hidden deep in the Pinelands off the main roadways, where he bales sphagnum moss and makes charcoal from old pine trees. Wasovich is known for the colorful description given of him by author John McPhee in his beloved book, *The Pine Barrens*, first published in 1968 when Wasovich was just a teenager.

ecological gem in itself) in southern Ocean and southeastern Burlington Counties. McPhee's book just might have been the reason the Pinelands exist today. His words of warning were heeded, as evidenced by the fact that the federal government and the State of New Jersey took major steps to preserve it. In 1978, Congress approved the National Parks and Recreation Act (NPRA), which established Pinelands National Reserve (the first in the country), and in 1979, the State of New Jersey Pinelands Commission was established. The Pinelands Comprehensive Management Plan, as required by the NPRA, was approved in 1981.

The Pinelands National Reserve is slightly larger than the New Jersey Pinelands area, as it protects certain coastal areas as well as the interior region. The map entitled "New Jersey Pinelands Management Areas" from the Pinelands Commission defines the New Jersey Pinelands, with the additional National Reserve area clearly indicated by diagonal lines. The National Reserve encompasses over 1.1 million acres.

In 1983, the Pinelands was designated a U.S. Biosphere Reserve by UNESCO (United Nations Educational, Scientific and Cultural Organization), and in 1988, it was named an International Biosphere Reserve. Yes, the New Jersey Pinelands is an amazingly rich and ecologically significant place on this earth!

FLORA AND FAUNA

It is important to understand and respect the plants and animals of the Pinelands. There are more than 850 species of plants here, some of which are extremely endangered. Possibly the most beautiful is the Pine Barrens gentian, a bright blue flower that blooms in September, but others such as the swamp pink, white-fringed orchid (yes, there are several species of orchids in the Pinelands) and the bog asphodel are equally resplendent. Perhaps the most interesting, however, are the carnivorous plants. Not to worry, they are hardly large enough to devour a mouse, much less a human, so there's no fear of being sucked into a monstrous pitcher plant or super sundew. These plants adapted to the nutrient-poor soils of the Pines by ingesting small insects to ensure proper nutrition—quite an amazing feat!

It is important to tread lightly when in the Pine Barrens so a threatened or endangered plant isn't accidentally crushed. Trails abound both in the uplands and in wetlands, where viewing of these plants can be accomplished without danger of accidentally stepping on them. In many cases, however,

A lady's slipper orchid (*cypripedium acaule*), one of almost a dozen orchids that grow in the New Jersey Pinelands. Many of these flowers are endangered; some plants' only known habitat is the New Jersey Pinelands.

they are flourishing in places seldom traveled by humans or at least deep within the Pines, where it is difficult to disturb them.

While there are over almost five hundred species of animals in the Pinelands, including mammals, birds, reptiles, amphibians and fish, very few pose any real danger to humans. Most animals of the Pine Barrens are rarely seen by the casual traveler. One of the larger mammals, the white-tailed deer, is very common and can often be seen from a distance grazing along the roadside or walking through the woods, but they are timid and will dart off if approached. Coyotes are rarely seen, but their haunting howl can sometimes be heard at night—a sound that has terrified more than a few wilderness campers. While it has been reported that black bear and bobcat, or their tracks, have been spotted in the Pine Barrens, they have not established long-term residence here.

The resident animals in the Pine Barrens to fear most may well be the smaller ones. For example, although considered an endangered species in New Jersey, the timber rattlesnake can be found in the Pine Barrens, though it is very reclusive. Regardless, care should always be taken when walking deep in the woods among deadwood, old foundations from abandoned ghost towns and other hideouts that snakes call home.

There are a few insects that can inflict poisonous venom as well; the black widow and brown recluse spiders can be found here, but neither is particularly common. If found at all, these spiders, like the rattlers, will often be hiding under old artifacts such as bricks or concrete, so once again, it's wise to keep a distance from this type of potential habitat. Much more common in the Pines are ticks, chiggers and what many say should be the state bird: the mosquito. Add to this mix some biting flies of various sizes and colors, and you've got a good reason to use insect repellent and wear long pants tucked into your socks if you wander into the woods.

New Jersey's location along the Atlantic Coastal Flyway makes it an ideal location for birders. The Pinelands National Reserve protects much of this area. In fact, Cape May, New Jersey, is ranked in the top ten of bird-watching regions in North America.

Speaking of state birds, New Jersey's is the eastern goldfinch, but if you're a birder, you will be thrilled to know that there are over three hundred varieties of birds in the Pinelands, ranging in size from the diminutive ruby-throated hummingbird to egrets, great blue herons and the majestic bald eagle. There are many excellent locations for birding throughout the Pinelands; New Jersey's location along the Atlantic Coastal Flyway makes it a prime location for birding, especially during spring and fall migration.

Sugar-Sand Roads

Perhaps you've heard the phrase "sugar sand" as it relates to New Jersey's Pine Barrens but have always wondered what it really means. A bit of prehistoric history, hopefully not too painfully reminiscent of school days of old, will explain this. About 100 million years ago, the Atlantic Ocean repeatedly ebbed and flowed over the entire coastal plain where the Pinelands is located, leaving behind organic and geologic material, better known as—yes—"sugar sand." Inland, it's not quite as white as that of New Jersey's beautiful beaches, but it is sugar sand nonetheless. You may even find occasional seashell pieces many miles inland. On a moonlit night, the sand glows almost as white as snow. An amazing sight to see in the winter is a blueberry field where the branches of the blueberry bushes have turned bright red against the white sand.

Of course, this sand can be a bit of a problem for those who venture off the paved roads. Many are drawn to the miles and miles of sugar-sand roads that zigzag through the forest, but while many of those roads are hard-packed, often vehicles will get stuck deep in this sugar sand, which is a good reason not to venture too far off the main roadways unless you are prepared and know where you are going. The best time to explore these roads is during daylight, and it's important to remember that venturing out after a rain will result in getting stuck in flooded areas. It's often difficult to tell the depth of puddles until it's too late. While the main roads are generally easily traversed by a standard vehicle, it is recommended that four-wheel drive be used for extensive exploration.

Aquifer System

An important feature of the Pinelands is invisible but vital and a major reason for protecting this area. The Kirkwood-Cohansey aquifer system lies underneath the Pinelands and contains about seventeen trillion gallons of some of the purest water in the country, if not the world. A "trillion" is hard to visualize, but as an aid, picture the entire state of New Jersey (8,722 square miles) under ten feet of water and you'll get a rough idea of what seventeen trillion gallons looks like. This water supplies most residents of the Pinelands region with drinking water from both wells and municipal water supplies, as well as providing water for the Pine Barrens' beautiful rivers, streams and wetlands. Of course, it also supplies the native plants and animals with water too. Since it's a shallow system, it's especially important that measures are taken to protect it from contaminants and one of many reasons such strict regulations are in place to protect the Pinelands.

Early Industry in the Pines

While I'm not going to elaborate on history, it's a good idea to get a general idea of what went on in the past in and around the Pinelands before you begin to explore them. Later in this book, you'll learn a bit more about historical locations within each area, so this section is just an overview. There are dozens of excellent books by historians who have spent most of their lives studying this wonderful area; they are available at several locations throughout the Pinelands.

With its proximity to major waterways and cities, the early Pinelands region was once a bustling area not much different than it is today, at least along the coastal areas. The whaling industry, which began along the Jersey coast in the mid-1600s, precipitated a huge boat-building industry a few decades later that continues to this day. Beginning in the early eighteenth century, more towns sprouted up, many along the coast and waterways, with stage roads connecting them to one another and eventually to major colonial cities. Although traditional farming was difficult, lumbering flourished because of the abundance of forested land, especially pine, oak and cedar, which still thrive here due to the acidic soil. These trees were used in construction and boat building, as a heating source and more. The many streams and rivers throughout the area provided water power for sawmills.

When "bog iron" was discovered along the banks of the Pinelands' rivers and streams in the mid-1700s, the iron era began. During its heyday, the many furnaces throughout the Pines remained "in fire" seven days a week, twenty-four hours a day, from early spring until winter, when the ponds, created by man to supply water power as the water flowed over the dams, froze over. The abundance of pine trees provided colliers an ample source for making charcoal to fire the furnaces, and clam and oyster shells from the nearby bays provided flux for starting the fires. The iron era lasted about one hundred years, until the discovery of a superior quality iron ore in Pennsylvania. Also, the bog iron deposits in the Pinelands' rivers were depleted. However, with the plentiful sand in the region, glassmaking factories were built as an industry to replace the former iron industry and flourished for a while. In fact, the Mason jar was first designed and made in Crowleytown, located near Batsto on the Mullica River. Because of the iron content in the Pinelands sand, the glass made here had a green, blue or aqua tint, which became unpopular during that period. When the supply of wood needed for the glassmaking process was depleted late in the nineteenth century, the glass industry died out.

The sawmill at Historic Batsto Village within Wharton State Forest, situated at the dam of the beautiful Batsto Lake. Batsto River was harvested for its bog iron during the heyday of the iron era in the New Jersey Pinelands.

The remains of the paper mill at Harrisville are visible from just off the roadside on Route 679, across from Harrisville Lake. Harrisville was once a thriving town, resplendent with lovely homes and businesses and even gaslights along the streets. These remains, contained behind chain-link fencing to prevent vandalism, are about all that is left of this once-thriving town.

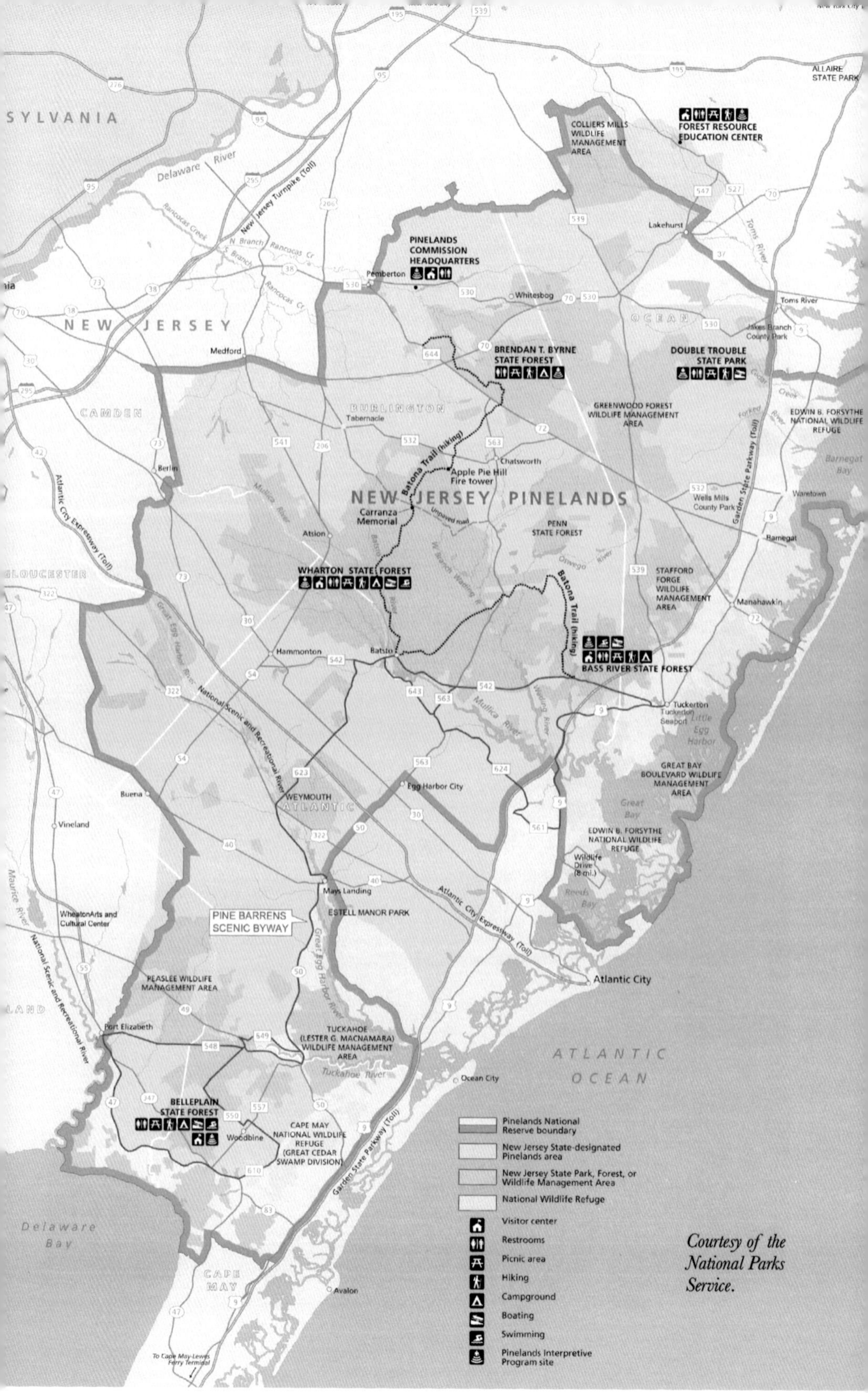

Courtesy of the National Parks Service.

Paper mills were also built in the Pines during this period. Wood from the forests, along with salt hay, provided the materials to make butcher paper at a number of paper mills, including Harrisville, a ghost town that during its heyday was quite resplendent.

Because of the use of pines, cedars and oaks for lumber, iron furnaces and heating, the heavily forested areas one sees today throughout the Pinelands were not always so lush. The rapid lumbering performed during this time depleted much of the forest. Even in the wetlands, cedar trees were harvested from the marshes for use in building. The access roads to these areas were lined with logs so that wagon wheels would not sink in the mud. These roads were called corduroy roads for their resemblance to the cloth of the same name.

The company towns once bustling with activities for the most part became ghost towns, with only a few surviving. Those who stayed learned to live off the land by farming cranberries and blueberries, harvesting sphagnum moss and pine cones and hunting. Many Pineys—then and now—worked both the land and the coastal waters. Clamming, crabbing, fishing and, in its day, whaling were coastal occupations undertaken by locals, though today, you may find that although most Pineys don't mind being labeled as Baymen, there are some Baymen who will vehemently deny being Pineys. What you will find today are many locals, whether Baymen or Pineys, who are proud of the tradition they carry on. As a result, there are many talented men, women and children in the Pinelands today who share their tradition of music, artistry, woodcarving, basket making, boat building, fishing, farming, house building, hunting and many other specialties that are unique to this magical region of America.

Part II

Northern Region

The northern region of the Pinelands, for the purposes of this book, ranges roughly from Island Beach State Park south of Seaside Heights/Seaside Park along the Atlantic coast; westward to Route 206 near Pemberton; north from just below Interstate 195; and southward to Route 72 and Route 530. This region can be easily accessed along the coastal area via the Garden State Parkway or Interstate 95/NJ Turnpike from the west.

Chapter 2

Lakehurst and Jackson

We're going to start our northern region tour from the Garden State Parkway in Brick Township, New Jersey. You're not technically in the official New Jersey or national delineation of the Pinelands, but a look around at the many pines (amid the commercial development that has taken place) will assure you that you are indeed within the Pine Barrens. Actually, for city dwellers, this starting point is probably a good one; after all, I'm not guiding you deep into Jersey Devil country—not quite yet, anyway!

Lakehurst Borough

Heading west on Route 70, you will pass quite a bit of development, including several adult communities. It seems that this clean Pine Barrens air is good for longevity, because there are over fifty adult communities in Ocean County alone. Continue on Route 70 for about eight miles until you reach the town of Lakehurst and the official boundary line of the New Jersey Pinelands. Stay on Route 70 past the small circle where Route 37, leading from Seaside Heights (yes, the location of the reality show *Jersey Shore*) and Toms River, terminates—New Jersey is famous for its traffic circles—and to the second circle where a small mall is located. Take it three-quarters of the way around to Union Avenue.

Driving east on Union Avenue, you will see the picturesque Lake Horicon on your right. In the late 1700s, the shoreline of Lake Horicon in what is now the borough of Lakehurst was home to the Federal Forge, the first iron forge in Ocean County. Known as Manchester until 1921, Lakehurst gained fame as a winter resort from the late nineteenth century to early in the twentieth century because of the luxurious Pine Tree Inn on Lake Horicon that was a popular spot for up to 150 guests, mostly from northern New Jersey and New York. It had a long sun porch, game rooms, fireplaces, tennis courts and even a small golf course. The lure was that the climate was much like Norfolk, Virginia, and the fresh pine air was recuperative to one's soul. The Pine Tree Inn was open from October through May for "rest and health," which included walks around the lake, hikes through the "pine woods" or ice skating on the lake's frozen waters.

Although the hotel is no longer in existence, the pristine sixty-four-acre spring-fed cedar water Lake Horicon remains a popular swimming spot, as well as a site for festivals, flea markets and craft shows for residents and visitors alike. If you visit in the summer, take a dip in the clear, cool lake—but remember that cedar water will turn a white bathing suit a lovely shade of pale yellow as a result of the iron and tannins in the water. A small road

The Lakehurst Historical Society headquarters is located in this church, the oldest Roman Catholic church in Ocean County, New Jersey.

runs along the east side of the lake, where lowbush blueberries can be found growing wild in early summer.

During the heyday of railroads, Lakehurst was also the site of one of the largest shop areas of the Central Railroad of New Jersey, with a roundhouse, old locomotive sheds and a passenger and freight station. The famed "Blue Comet," the popular train that ran from Jersey City to Atlantic City until 1941, made a regular stop here. For history buffs, the Lakehurst Historical Society is located on Center Street in the Old St. John's Church, the oldest Roman Catholic church in Ocean County. It contains a number of interesting artifacts, including some charred remnants from the *Hindenburg* and furnishings from the Pine Tree Inn. Since it is run by local volunteers, museum hours are limited, so it's best to call ahead if you plan to visit.

Lakehurst maintains much of its old-town charm along Union Avenue, where many large homes still line the street, as well as several of the adjoining streets (I particularly enjoy Church Street, one block south of Union Avenue).

Hangar No. 1 at Lakehurst Naval Air Engineering Station

Lakehurst is probably best known for Hangar No. 1, where the *Hindenburg* met its fate on May 6, 1937, at the Lakehurst Naval Air Engineering Station. Lakehurst Naval Air also has the distinction of being the first international airport in North America. Located on Route 547 north of Lakehurst, it's possible to view the landmark hangar from the roadway, where one of the navy's Blue Angels proudly stands guard at the gate.

The *Hindenburg*, the largest dirigible ever to fly, was almost 804 feet long—almost three times that of a football field—dwarfing a Boeing 707. The massive fiery explosion killed thirteen of thirty-six passengers, twenty-two of sixty-one crew members and one civilian. There were sixty-two survivors, though many suffered severe injuries. This tragedy signaled the end of the era of dirigibles. Before this flight, the massive airship had completed many round trips between Frankfurt, Germany, and Brazil.

Hangar No. 1, with measurements of 961 feet long by 350 feet wide by 200 feet high, was designated as a National Historic Landmark in 1968. Navy Lakehurst was originally known as Camp Kendrick, the U.S. Army's experimental site for chemical warfare technology, such as mustard gas, in the early twentieth century.

Lakehurst is home to the Chapel of the Air, adjacent to Lakehurst Naval Air Engineering Station. Stained-glass windows in the chapel depict the history of flight in fact and myth.

Access to the base is restricted for security reasons, but limited tours are available through the Navy Lakehurst Historical Society, with a minimum of two weeks' advance registration. Strict security measures are taken but well worth the wait. However, a worthwhile stop is the Cathedral of the Air, located on the westerly side of Route 547, south of the base entrance. It is a Gothic-style church built in the 1930s with eighteen exquisite stained-glass windows commemorating the history of flight, from the winged horse Pegasus to the dirigibles. While you can walk about the pine tree–flanked grounds of the chapel, it is only open for services on Sundays, though it is included in the Navy Lakehurst Historical Society's tour.

FOREST RESOURCE EDUCATION CENTER IN JACKSON TOWNSHIP

For those interested in forestry, a visit to the New Jersey Forest Resource Education Center, located on Don Connor Boulevard in Jackson, is in order. Here, you can visit the interpretive center and forest nursery. There are also miles of trails with informational kiosks, as well as a number of self-guided trails, including the Arboretum Trail, Forest Trail and Swamp Life Trail. Each has accompanying guide booklets. This 660-acre center run by the New Jersey Division of Parks and Forestry encourages forest stewardship, provides an excellent overview of typical Pine Barrens uplands and wetlands and is very child-friendly. Each October, a Fall Forestry Festival is held here, offering a variety of nature-related activities for all ages.

Rova Farm Resort and St. Vladimir's Russian Orthodox Memorial Church in Cassville

Just a few minutes from the Forest Resource Education Center is the Rova Farm Resort, developed as a Russian cultural center over seventy-five years ago. Located on Route 571, the resort runs an outdoor flea market in the parking lot and around the lake every Tuesday from 6:00 a.m. to 1:00 p.m., weather permitting. In season, up to one hundred vendors sell everything from antiques to fresh farm products. Adjacent to this site is a memorial to Russian author Alexander Pushkin, considered to be the founder of modern Russian literature.

Northern Ocean County's Pinelands is home to a Russian community. This is St. Vladimir's Russian Orthodox Church, located just off Route 547 in the Cassville section of Jackson Township.

Continue on Route 547/Cassville Road to see two churches representative of beautiful Russian architecture. The lower church, dedicated to the Protection of the Theotokos, or "mother of God," was the first operational church space of St. Vladimir's. This was because the construction of the upper, main temple was temporarily halted due to financial hardship. As a result, for nearly twenty years, the crypt church, which was entirely dug out by hand, *was* St. Vladimir's. When the upper temple was completed, the lower church was renamed for St. Olga. After an ancient, blackened icon "miraculously renewed itself" in the lower church and revealed itself to be the Protection of the Theotokos, the lower church was renamed. Today, the lower church is the final resting place for their Eminences, Archbishops Vitaly and Nikon, and serves as the worship space for services in English. Today, St. Vladimir's Russian Orthodox Church, with its golden onion dome, is a stunning example of Russian architecture.

Return to Route 571 and turn right on Route 528. Much of the area you see here is part of Collier's Mills Wildlife Management Area, almost thirteen thousand acres of wilderness area protected by the state that preserve the wildlife habitat of the area. There are over one hundred such areas throughout New Jersey, ranging in size from just over a half acre to the thirty-thousand-acre Greenwood Forest tract in the Pinelands.

When you reach Route 539 (about five miles from Cassville), turn left and continue on to Route 70. Along Route 539, you will be traveling through Maguire–Fort Dix Army Air Force Base, which is located within the Pinelands. Note the chain-link fencing and restricted roads; if you're lucky, you'll glimpse a large cargo plane low in the sky, preparing to land nearby.

Once you reach the Route 70 intersection, you can return to Lakehurst and the Garden State Parkway or extend your tour.

Chapter 3
Brendan T. Byrne State Forest

Whitesbog Village

Turn west on Route 70 and continue through the Pinelands to Route 530. Just about a mile down on the right will be a sign for Whitesbog Village, which is located within Brendan T. Byrne State Forest. This is a dirt road (Whitesbog Road) but is safe for travel without need of four-wheel drive.

Whitesbog has a fascinating history. Currently run by the nonprofit Whitesbog Preservation Trust, it is the home of the first cultivated blueberries, which are those big juicy berries that are available in early summer, usually from mid-June to Late July.

Young Elizabeth White, daughter of the Whitesbog cranberry farm owner Joseph J. White, wanted to use the land surrounding the cranberry bogs where wild (lowbush) blueberries were growing to cultivate and grow blueberries but didn't have any scientific background. In 1911, she persuaded her father to reach out to Fredrick V. Colville, who was researching blueberry cultivation. Mr. Colville agreed to perform his research at Whitesbog. Five years later, they managed to cultivate and produce blueberries for sale. Elizabeth had actually hired the local Pineys to search out the largest blueberries in the area; those who found them were additionally rewarded with a hybrid blueberry bush in their name, most of which are still being produced today.

Today, Whitesbog still produces blueberries and cranberries, and Suningive, Elizabeth's home until her death in 1954, is still standing, as are

Whitesbog Village in the northern Pinelands is the home of Elizabeth White, who was instrumental in developing the large cultivated blueberries we enjoy today. Suningive, her home at Whitesbog, is available for tours on special occasions, such as the annual Blueberry Festival held each June. The general store, shown here, is the base for a number of festivities and tours that are offered throughout the year.

a number of other buildings in the company village. The General Store displays a number of interesting artifacts and photos and offers a variety of items for purchase. It is a good idea to call ahead for hours, especially off-season, as the shop is run mostly by volunteers and is open on weekends only.

A five-mile self-guided driving tour past cranberry bogs and blueberry fields is available, but it is on a sugar-sand road, so it's not advisable to take the tour during wet conditions, as the shoulders of the roads across the bogs can become soft and unstable. A number of brochures containing self-guided walking tours, such as the Old Bog Nature Trail, are available, and special tours and talks are offered during Whitesbog events. One feature that is fun for all is the monthly Full Moon Hike, in which a trained naturalist leads the group around the bogs and fields. There is a small fee, but it is well worth it for the excitement of a nighttime hike in the Pines.

New Jersey is a major producer of cultivated blueberries; in fact, it usually ranks in the top five states in annual production. That is quite a feat for the fifth-smallest state in size and second in population density in the Union. Each year, the annual Whitesbog Blueberry Festival is held here, usually on the last Saturday in June, to celebrate the annual harvest. Everything blueberry is available—blueberry pies, muffins, ice cream, cake, fresh blueberries and even blueberry bushes. There's lots more, too: local Piney musicians provide wonderful entertainment; vendors and nonprofit agencies have tables with information about the Pinelands, as well as a variety of interesting items for sale, especially locally handmade arts and crafts; and wagon tours of the fields are available for picking blueberries, as well as tours of the village. Each year brings more exciting additions.

Return to Route 70 westbound. Although there is an entrance to Brendan T. Byrne State Forest on the left, I suggest proceeding to the traffic circle (yes, another circle!) and taking it three-quarters of the way around to Route 72. The "official" entrance to the forest with visitors' center will be a mile ahead on the left. Stop in to the center for some information to help you navigate this 36,647-acre Pinelands forest.

The forest was first known as Lebanon State Forest, named for the Lebanon Glass Works, which produced high-quality window glass here between 1851 and 1857. The fine white sand and abundance of trees used for charcoal made it a great success—that is, until the supply of trees ran out, due in large part to poor planning. The factory was abandoned and overtaken by renewed forest. In 2002, it was renamed to honor former governor Brendan T. Byrne, who was a major factor in the establishment of protective laws and regulations for the New Jersey Pinelands. Here, you'll find seventy-nine individual tenting and trailer campsites, group campsites able to facilitate up to one hundred campers, three cabins and three yurts (round, cabin-like tents with screened windows, wooden doors and Plexiglas skylights). Picnic tables and grills are available throughout the park. Over twenty-five miles of marked trails are located here, including part of the famous Batona Trail, which traverses the Pinelands from Ongs' Hat just north of Route 70 all the way to its terminus in Bass River State Forest, for a total of just over fifty miles. Batona is an abbreviated name for Back to Nature. It was developed by nature-loving volunteers, who perform the majority of the maintenance on the trail. The pink blazes marking the trail are seen throughout Wharton State Forest.

One of the prettiest vistas in this forest may well be from the shores of Pakim Pond, once a reservoir for the nearby cranberry bogs. It is generally believed that the name Pakim comes from Delaware Indian chief Pakimintzen, who apparently had a penchant for the wild cranberries that grew in the area and distributed them at tribal peace feasts. Three furnished cabins are also located along its shores. These cabins are very

Insider's Tip: If all the walking at Brendan T. Byrne State Forest has you hungry, then upon your exit back onto Route 72 East, stop by Mayo's Halfway House about a half mile down the road on the right. This is not a fancy restaurant; quite the contrary. It is *very* rustic, with mismatched tables and chairs and some bar stools with a significant wobble, but it has good food, and most of it, such as the mozzarella sticks, is handmade by the resident chef, who, by the way, takes great pride in his knowledge of the area. Mayo's has been around for many years, and both the chef and owner enjoy talking about its history. In fact, inside Mayo's menu is the following, written by its owner, Andrew Emmons:

A Bit of History As We Know It

Records on the actual building and owners are scarce, if not non-existent, prior to 1934 when prohibition ended and Mayo's received its liquor license. (There's hundreds of stories about what happened here during prohibition, but none suitable for print.) Rumor has it the log cabin was built with the cedar cut down to clear Lakehurst Naval Base.

Jack Bond, the earliest proprietor, named Mayo's "Bond's Halfway House." Jack sold his bar to Frankie Mayo sometime in the early '50's (although both were heavy gamblers and it's quite possible, judging from the $1 sale price, that Jack lost it to Frankie in a poker game.)

Frankie and his wife Grace advertised Mayo's as Frankie Mayo's Halfway House and Motel "where A Sandwich was a meal." In 1971 they sold the bar to Helen and Paul Lally from Long Beach Island. Helen and Paul along with their incredibly large family (12 kids) worked Mayo's extremely successfully for 32 years (most of you will remember Chrissy and Eddie.) In March of 2003 they decided to sell to long time employee (14 years) Andrew Emmons.

Andrew started at Mayo's in the summer of 1989 as a dishwasher and waiter and was behind the bar, usually Sunday nights, for the better part of 10 years. Knowing the business from an employee standpoint was easy, but ownership? Well that would take an entire page. Andrew brought some new ideas with him (including an extensive renovation), along with keeping many of Mayo's longtime traditions including the name and the revival of the baby deer. He has committed himself to the former owners' vision of a comfortable place that people can call home.

So if you want a taste of real Pinelands culture, stop at Mayo's for a sandwich or a meal.

Pakim Pond in Brendan T. Byrne State Forest is a tranquil place, as this photo shows. Look more closely, however, and you will find its shores teeming with life. Frogs, dragonflies, tiny sundews and other unusual plants dot the landscape.

popular, and advance reservation is needed to rent them, but with their location on the banks of this beautiful pond, it's easy to understand why.

Pakim Pond is a botanist's delight, with its huge variety of plants, some of which are classified as endangered or threatened. Look carefully at the banks and you might even see some carnivorous plants, such as the delicate sundew. If you're very quiet as you gently walk along the waterline, you might see some resident amphibians. If dragons and damsels are more to your liking, this is a veritable haven for these gorgeous flying insects, one of the most ancient on earth. Remember, they do *not* bite or sting and are harmless to humans—quite the contrary, since their diet includes a number of pests such as mosquitoes.

Chapter 4
Barnegat

The Pygmy Pine Plains

Continue east on Route 72 for several miles and you will begin to notice something strange about the oak and pine trees along the side of the roadway—they're shrinking! This odd phenomenon occurs in only a few places in the world, but the New Jersey Pinelands' pygmy pines are probably the best known. The two Pine Plains within the New Jersey Pinelands total about 12,400 acres. The section along Route 72 is referred to as the West Pine Plains; the East Pine Plains are located in Warren Grove (central region), where a 2007 forest fire burned over 17,000 acres of forest, most of it the pygmy pines.

Pitch pines and blackjack oaks, found throughout the Pinelands at heights of up to eighty feet, grow in these pygmy Pine Plains to an average of about four feet tall. Scientists have studied this strange growth phenomenon for years; it seems that the best theory is that plains such as these are exposed to more wind and drying conditions and, as a result, more fire. As a self-preservation measure, these trees have evolved to regenerate fairly rapidly after a fire. To do so, they have developed a deeper root system to draw needed nutrients for their regrowth. Also, many (though not all) of the pine cones are serotinous, which means that they have the ability to adapt to a variety of situations. This means that these cones do not open to release seeds until they have been exposed to extreme heat, such as a fire.

The dwarf pines and oaks along this sugar-sand road through the pygmy pines is a good example of just how small these trees are.

This pine cone is a good example of its serotinous nature, which ensures survival of the species. Taken the day after the fire of 2007, the cone had opened fully in response to the intense heat in order to release the seeds, which can be seen near the base of the cone.

Cedar Bridge Tavern

Continue on Route 72 east to Old Halfway Road, a hard-packed sugar-sand road on the right. Not many people are aware that the last skirmish of the American Revolution occurred right here in the Pinelands, on Old Halfway Road in Barnegat Township. Every year on December 27, the reenactment is performed at the still-standing Cedar Bridge Tavern and narrated by the Ocean County historian, who is dressed in official Revolutionary regalia.

The sign erected here by the Ocean County Board of Chosen Freeholders to commemorate Ocean County's role in the Revolutionary War reads:

> *December 27, 1782—After searching several days for the notorious Capt. John Bacon, Capt. Richard Shreve of the Burlington County Light Horse and Capt. Edward Thomas of the Mansfield Militia stopped with their men to refresh themselves near here at the Cedar Bridge Tavern. Bacon and his band of loyalists surprised the militia and blocked their escape. As the militia gained the advantage, they were fired upon unexpectedly by a party of locals who came to Bacon's aid and provided a diversion that allowed Bacon to escape. Among the patriots, one was killed and four were wounded. Four loyalists were also wounded, including Captain Bacon.*

A Patriot takes aim during the reenactment held each year on December 27, the anniversary of the last skirmish of the American Revolutionary War, at the Cedar Bridge Tavern in Barnegat.

Ocean County purchased the tavern and the surrounding 5 acres in 2008; the New Jersey Conservation Foundation owns the remaining 195 acres. The tavern's former owner maintains life rights to the building, which is his home, and even has the original bar. If you do drive past this historical site, observe it from the street; use discretion and respect its resident's rights, as the building is not open to the public.

Return to Route 72 and turn right. If you are considering an overnight stay on the ocean, Route 72 will take you right onto Long Beach Island, a beautiful seventeen-mile stretch of barrier island on the Atlantic Ocean, with several nice lodging facilities and dozens of wonderful restaurants. Additionally, en route to Long Beach Island are many malls with the usual conglomeration of chain stores and restaurants, located along Route 72 in Stafford Township, as well as a Holiday Inn. A campground/RV park is also located just off Route 72. However, I'm going to guide you into Barnegat, just north of Stafford.

From Route 72, turn onto Route 554/West Bay Avenue. As you travel east, about a mile and a half down on the right, you'll see a pretty little pond. An old-timer who has since passed once told me this was named Turpentine Pond, "though I don't rightly know why, to tell the truth" (although one must imagine that at one time, turpentine was extracted from the pines nearby). Each time I drive by that pond, I think of him and the wonderful stories he told me over the years. Most locals, or Pineys, will gladly talk to you once they know you respect their heritage and are genuinely interested, so be sure to listen. Their stories are steeped in history and very entertaining; if you are lucky enough to hear one, consider it a special occasion.

Cloverdale Farm County Park

If you want to see a cranberry farm "the way it used to be," continue driving about two miles, past the several adult communities that have been built in the Pinelands' "regional growth zone," and then look on the right side of the roadway for the brown wooden sign with Cloverdale Farm County Park engraved in white letters. This is a hard-packed dirt road; take it about a mile to its end. You will reach several large cranberry bogs and a few old farm buildings, including a sorting house. (The original homestead burned

The old cranberry sorting barn at Cloverdale Farm County Park, as seen from across the naturalized bogs that were the heart of this working cranberry farm in Barnegat.

to the ground in 2010.) This eighty-acre farm was a working cranberry farm for almost one hundred years. Its former owner wanted the land preserved and not developed, as the adjacent land has been, so she sold it—at a financial loss—to the government for preservation as "open space" instead of selling to developers. Since its purchase by Ocean County, the bogs have been allowed to return to a natural state, and in late fall, supervised dry picking of cranberries is permitted. (You'll read more about New Jersey's cranberry industry and dry harvest v. wet harvest later.) A number of weekend outdoor programs and walks are offered here at little or no cost. There are trails all the way around the bogs, so if you have time, walk out and around them. During any season, you'll be rewarded with beautiful views and an assortment of wildlife, and from spring through autumn, you'll find a plethora of wildflowers.

Historic District

After visiting Cloverdale, stay on Route 554 for about three miles, past the hustle and bustle of the Garden State Parkway commercial area (the Garden State Parkway runs north–south through New Jersey's east coastal area and for the most part is the eastern boundary of the state-designated Pinelands) and to the Bay Avenue–Route 9 area. Over the past several years, Barnegat has grown immensely, but this is the historic district of town, and you should take the time to explore it. Many of the Victorian homes in Barnegat were once the residences of ship captains; in fact, some have widow's walks, small rooftop balconies where wives could look out to sea in hopes of seeing their husbands' ships returning to port. A good example is the well-known Cox House, on the northwest corner of Route 9 and Bay Avenue, built by Captain Billy and Marietta Cox. Currently listed on the State and National Register of Historic Places, this Colonial Revival home was the first house in Barnegat to have electricity and running water. On the southeast corner of Route 9 and East Bay Avenue is the Gold Duster, currently an art gallery featuring the work of regional artists and crafters. This building was painstakingly restored by its current owner. It is believed to have once been a carriage stop for visitors to the area. A bit farther east is another captain's house that is said to be haunted—but there are many of these in this region. A number of antique shops are also located here and along Route 9; in fact, the Route 9 corridor in Ocean, Atlantic and Cape May Counties has been dubbed "Antique Alley."

The Cox House at the intersection of Route 9 and Bay Avenue is a Barnegat landmark.

Perrine Boat Works was opened in 1900 in Barnegat by J.H. Perrine, who specialized in building the world-renowned Barnegat Bay Sneak Box, a twelve-foot-long rowboat used for duck hunting that was easy to navigate, enabling hunters to sneak up on ducks. This popular boat was also used for pleasure boating. In its day, over 3,500 boats were built in this small structure. The old building, which was once the home of the Barnegat Primary School, still exists; in fact, even the sign is still visible. It is located on School Street.

A few restaurants are located in the historic district, including Doyle's Pour House, Spiaggia e Luna and Sweet Jenny's. Sweet Jenny's is located in what was once the Hurricane House on East Bay Avenue. This building is a quaint 1900s soda shop, renovated to meet today's restaurant needs but retaining the charm of yesteryear, complete with penny candy. It also was a frequent stop for "Barnegat Pete," a deer lovingly adopted by a local family. Pete lived in Barnegat between 1935 and 1945 after being rescued from a forest fire as a fawn. He would occasionally walk through town looking for handouts and frequently stopped at what was then Brower's Drug Store for free ice cream. Pete was eventually donated to the Philadelphia Zoo, but years later, when visited by his former caretakers, he ran to the fence when he heard the call, "Hey, Petey!" If you stop in at Sweet Jenny's, you'll even see some photos of Pete on the wall.

Henry Hudson named the area Barende-gat, a Dutch term for an inlet with breakers, when he first came to the area in 1609. By the 1750s, several families had built homes here. In 1767, the Quaker Friends Meeting House, the oldest church in Barnegat and third oldest in Ocean County, was built. The church is still standing, and services are still held each Sunday morning. It's located at 614 East Bay Avenue and flanked by an old cemetery with interesting grave markers. About a quarter mile east is Heritage Village, with four restored buildings and three smaller structures. It has a number of interesting artifacts inside its buildings but is only open Saturdays from 10:00 a.m. to 4:00 p.m. between Memorial Day and Labor Day.

The original Perrine Boat Works, originally owned by J.H. Perrine, was located within this building in the historic district of Barnegat. The sign reads, "Perrine Boat Works, Builder of the Barnegat Bay Sneak Box. Repair work done. Garveys Built. Box 18 Brook St., John C. Chadwick, Owner." Today, a replica of this boat shop is located at Tuckerton Seaport, about twenty minutes south.

INSIDER'S TIP: To see what a boat-building shop looks like, visit nearby Tuckerton Seaport (Part II), where a replica of the Perrine Boat Works was constructed. You can watch master boat builders applying their expertise on boats being built on weekends and selected weekdays.

BAYSHORE AREA

Continuing on East Bay Avenue, it becomes Bayshore Drive, and the reason is obvious. This road runs parallel to the Barnegat Bay, with a number of marinas and waterfront homes at the shoreline and lining the many lagoons. A stop at the municipal dock will reward you with a view of the bay and of Ol' Barney standing guard at the northern tip of Long Beach Island. Ol' Barney, by the way, is the local name for Barnegat Lighthouse, located in the town of Barnegat Light. It is a working lighthouse standing 172 feet tall that was first lit in 1859. Although just outside the borders of the National Pinelands Reserve, the lighthouse is situated within Barnegat Lighthouse State Park, across the inlet from Island Beach State Park, which is part of the reserve. Barnegat Lighthouse State Park also features a 1,033-foot-long concrete walkway along the jetty, which is a great spot for bird-watching and fishing; a maritime forest trail; a picnic area with tables; and an interpretive center.

Barnegat Lighthouse, or "Ol' Barney," located at Barnegat Lighthouse State Park on the northern tip of Long Beach Island, a barrier island adjacent to the Pinelands National Reserve in the Ocean County area.

About a half mile after the road bends west again, look for a brown wooden sign on the left indicating

Edwin B. Forsythe National Wildlife Refuge. This is a small part of the entire refuge, which has a total of over forty-seven thousand acres, most of which is tidal salt meadow and marshland with shallow coves and bays, perfect for migrating and breeding waterfowl alike. The refuge is located at various locations along New Jersey's coastal areas in Atlantic and Ocean Counties. There is parking for a few cars here, with a boardwalk that is a short walk to an observation platform where in season you may spot herons, egrets and other shore and wading birds in this six-hundred-acre impoundment.

Barnegat Rail Trail

Barnegat is the starting point for the more than fifteen-mile-long rail-to-trail project undertaken by Ocean County. It is a level, solid surface amid the pines, perfect for walking, jogging or bicycling. This greenway was once the rail route of the Barnegat Branch Division of the Central Railroad of

The Barnegat Branch Rail Trail is a greenway that was developed along the old Barnegat Branch Division of the Central Railroad of New Jersey line, paralleling Route 9 from Barnegat Township. It will ultimately cover 15.6 miles to Toms River Township. It's used by walkers, joggers and bicyclists; dogs on leashes are also welcomed.

New Jersey. Access points are well marked from either East Bay Avenue or Barnegat Boulevard. It has access points in several areas and benches along the trails for drinking in the clear Pinelands air. Along the way are the remains from the old railroad turntable and water tower. This area is a good place to spot a number of birds and flowers, especially near the creek that can be seen from the trail. From Bayshore Drive, cross Route 9; rail trail signs and a parking area for the rail trail will be ahead on the right.

Chapter 5
Waretown

Once a sleepy coastal town and outside the New Jersey Pinelands but within the Pinelands National Reserve, Waretown has seen much growth, especially along the Route 9 corridor, and as a result, it has become somewhat of a low-key summer tourist destination, especially for boaters. Despite its growth, Waretown is a charming town with a nautical flavor and significant Pinelands appeal. With its location directly across from the Barnegat Inlet that opens to the Atlantic Ocean, it has numerous marinas that host boats of all sizes, from small motorized rowboats perfect to rent for a day of crabbing to huge cabin cruisers and fishing boats used for multi-day deep-sea fishing for tuna, blues or even shark.

Once known as Waier Creek and Waier Mills, after the mill owned by Abraham Waier in 1739, the name eventually evolved into Waretown. The political name of the area is actually Ocean Township, which includes Waretown, Brookville, Dog Town, Pebble Beach and several other neighborhoods that compose the entire township. Waretown has two old cemeteries. The largest is Cedar Grove Cemetery on Bryant Road, which was founded in 1861. It has about five hundred graves and is still being used today.

Albert Music Hall/Pinelands Cultural Society

Returning east on Route 532 will bring you to Albert Music Hall in Waretown. (Once you have crossed the Garden State Parkway, you have left the New Jersey–designated portion of the Pinelands but are still in the

Pinelands National Reserve.) Located at 131 Wells Mills Road (Route 532), this nationally known bluegrass-country music venue has an interesting history. In the 1970s, deep in the Pines of Waretown, brothers Joe and George Albert would invite friends to their home, which became known as the Old Home Place, to play their musical instruments and sing every week. It became a regular event for musicians from all around the area. After George died, it became too much for Joe, who was then in his eighties, so the get-togethers ceased. The musicians missed it so much that they rented a building on Route 9 in Waretown—where the post office now stands—and the gatherings went on every Saturday night, but this time with an audience happy to pay the small admission charged to cover expenses. Tragedy struck in 1992, when Albert Music Hall was destroyed by fire, but that didn't deter the musicians who had formed the Pinelands Cultural Society; they still gathered outside the remains to play until the local elementary school opened its doors to them. After raising funds, ground was broken in 1996 for a brand-new Albert Music Hall at its current location. It opened in January 1997 with over one thousand fans in attendance.

Jim Murphy and the Pine Barons perform at a number of big functions in the Pinelands. Here, the group is performing at the Pine Barrens Jamboree. In 2007, Jim Murphy became the first New Jersey musician to be inducted into the Old Time Country Music Hall of Fame. He has written such lyrical songs as "Chatsworth Town," "Forked River Mountains," "Polka in the Pines" and "Lenni-Lenape."

Many Pinelands restaurants offer a plethora of fresh seafood, such as this raw bar offering up oysters, clams, shrimp and crabs.

Today, music rings out every Saturday at 7:30 p.m. Also on site is the Pickin' Shed, where musicians are welcome to bring their instruments and play along. On any given night, you might hear guitars, banjoes, fiddles, mandolins, harmonicas, dulcimers and even spoons and washtubs, as these musicians from all over the region strive to preserve the classic bluegrass and country music of days gone by.

Just around the corner on Route 9 is the landmark Lighthouse Tavern. This old building was built as a stagecoach stop in the 1800s. Through a series of owners, it became Lyon's Inn, Lion's Inn, Lighthouse Inn and finally Lighthouse Tavern, where today good food and drinks are served in a pub atmosphere. Old photos line the walls near the bar area. Families are welcomed here before 9:00 p.m. Entertainment is provided on weekends, and a raw seafood bar is usually offered on Sunday afternoons, including clams, oysters, shrimp and crab.

Wells Mills County Park

Wells Mills County Park, located at 905 Wells Mills Road (Route 532), is a great destination for seeing a typical Pinelands ecosystem up close and personal. Within Wells Mills' borders are over 1,600 acres of uplands and wetlands, a 34-acre lake and a lovely three-story Nature Center offering a great display floor, a library and the third-level Elizabeth Meirs Morgan Observation Deck, dedicated to honor the longtime Ocean County naturalist and conservationist. An assortment of dioramas on the main level of the Nature Center portray wildlife in the Pines, and changing displays may feature cranberry farming, forest fire fighting or other significant events of the Pinelands. The Visitors' Center has a large porch overlooking the lake, where numerous bird feeders bring feathered friends year-round. A stairway to the third-floor observation area is flanked with photos and drawings of interest to anyone who enjoys nature, and once there, the view of the lake is just gorgeous. This lake, like all lakes in the Pinelands, is not a naturally made one but was dammed up many years ago in order to provide power for the two mills on the property (hence the name Wells Mills, not Wells Mill). Of course, the current dam is not the original; it was replaced several years ago by Ocean County. In season, canoe rentals are available for a nominal fee; paddles and safety gear are included. Swimming is not allowed here, although probably the greatest things to fear in this serene lake are the noisy geese and occasional snapping turtles that may show up.

Miles of marked trails of varying difficulty are available, including the VIP—Visually Impaired Persons—trail. A cord marked with knots guides the VIP around a short loop trail. At each knot, the visitor plays a recorded message of what is at that knot and can often reach out to touch what might be at that knot, such as the bark of a pine tree. The short Tree ID

The Nature Center at Wells Mills County Park stands grandly overlooking a pristine thirty-four-acre lake.

trail, only one-third of a mile long and marked with red blazes, will lead you to the old hunting lodge on the lake. While the lodge is not open to the public for safety reasons, just a walk around it conjures up images of late nights with hunting buddies on the rear porch overlooking the lake, telling tall tales of the Pines.

One of the many colorful stories of the Pines was that of the Wells Mills Frog Farm and Tom the giant frog. The story began back in 1968 with four locals out-telling one another's tales about the farm to a local radio DJ who had recently moved to the region from Brooklyn. The four men swore the frogs at Wells Mills had grown so big due to the quantity of mosquitoes they ate. They packed eight or ten cases a night with four to six frogs per case, to be shipped to the famous Fulton Fish Market in New York City. Each case, according to the jokesters, weighed in at about one hundred pounds. Tom, a particularly large specimen, was their "pet frog," but he had broken the chain and escaped. That chain hangs in the cabin to this day.

The hunting lodge at Wells Mills County Park was once owned by Cliff Oakley, a jovial, rosy-cheeked Piney with a knack for telling tales (some of them quite tall) who has passed on and is missed by all. Although closed to the public for safety reasons, a walk around it is a nostalgic glance at the property's past.

The chain used to restrain the legendary "Tom the Giant Frog" still hangs inside the hunting lodge to the right of the woodstove.

One of those fun-loving men owned the cabin. Whenever a youngster came to visit, the charming and personable Cliff Oakley (an old friend of mine who has passed on) would bring out a small box and, with a twinkle in his eye, would tell the child—or even an unsuspecting adult—that if he'd like to see "Chainsaw," to quietly look into the front opening. Then he would spring open the lid, and a big piece of an old animal hide would fly out, sending the child (or adult) into shrieks of fear and, eventually, laughter.

Today, the gentle spirit of years past still exists as one strolls around the picturesque cabin, whose roof is colorfully covered with bright green moss. Take a walk to the floating dock at the edge of the thirty-four-acre lake just behind the cabin to enjoy the peaceful vista it offers. You're also likely to see a flock of geese and any number of other birds in the water or in the skies above. The Macri (White) Trail nearby leads along the water's edge for a short distance, and if you pay attention, you might see the remains of an old corduroy road, made many years ago by lining up cedar logs along the roadway as natural pavers of sorts so that wagons carrying the cedar harvest wouldn't get stuck in the wetlands mud.

Wells Mills County Park is home to the annual Pine Barrens Jamboree. Every October on the second Saturday of the month, Pineys and visitors gather to hear music provided by the Albert Music Hall/Pinelands Cultural Society. The songs go on all day long "under the tent," but also at the jamboree are local artists and crafters, including woodcarvers, basket weavers, artists, writers, farmers, beekeepers and more offering their wares for sale. Mini-tours are available, frequently to Cloverdale Farm County Park, where the cranberries are usually ripe at this time of year, or the nearby Forked River

Left: The Jersey Devil occasionally makes cameo appearances at the Pine Barrens Jamboree, held each year in October at Wells Mills County Park in Waretown. Although this fellow looks quite peaceful, his legend does not depict him as quite so pleasant.

Below: Each fall at the Pine Barrens Jamboree, freshly dry-harvested cranberries are offered for sale by Erin Headley of Headley Farms in West Creek.

Mountains. There are arts and crafts and educational fun for children, lots of food vendors and demonstrations…the list goes on and on. And you never know when Smokey Bear or the Jersey Devil might show up!

The Pine Barrens Jamboree is free, and shuttle buses are available for overflow parking. This is one of those places in the Pine Barrens where you can go to get a true taste of Piney life without spending anything—unless you decide to make a purchase or two!

Lighthouse Center for Natural Resource Education

Once a camp for visually impaired, this property is owned by the New Jersey Department of Environmental Protection, Division of Fish and Wildlife, and is managed by the Natural Resource Education Foundation (NREF). It's situated on almost two hundred acres of diverse coastal habitat on the Barnegat Bay and includes a maritime forest, salt marsh, tidal streams and a

The Natural Resource Education Foundation at the Lighthouse Center, 194 acres located on the Barnegat Bay in Waretown and within the Pinelands National Reserve, was once a camp for the blind. It was purchased by the New Jersey Trust for Public Land and transferred to the New Jersey Department of Environmental Education, Division of Fish and Wildlife, and is now used primarily as an educational facility.

freshwater impoundment. It is used primarily by school and scout groups for educational purposes, marine research and as an eco-tour site. A number of professional development offerings for educators are also available. As there are a number of cabins and a lodge on site and available to groups as rentals, many multiday retreats take place here. Public events are run here several times a year, including Waterfowling and Family Fun Day, Artisans Retreat and the Basketry and Fiber Bash, when gates to this lovely reserve are open to the public. Those interested in a tour can contact the center directly.

Chapter 6

Forked River, Bayville and Beachwood

Forked River Mountains

I have often heard the question, "Where are the mountains?" asked by visitors (and even some residents) to this area. Coming from almost anywhere else, even central New Jersey, most people are amused at our "mountains" in the Pines. But the Forked River Mountains do exist. Consisting of over twenty thousand acres in the Pinelands of central Ocean County, with Wells Mills County Park, Double Trouble State Park, Route 539 and the Garden State Parkway as its rough boundaries, this area is blessed with pristine forests and streams, as well as a large variety of flora and fauna. The "mountains" are actually a pair of sand/gravel hills, with the larger one, East Mountain, looming a lofty 184 feet into the sky. From its peak, one can see Ol' Barney (Barnegat Lighthouse) to the east and historic Hangar No. 1 at the Lakehurst Naval Engineering Center to the northwest, as well as the seemingly endless vista of the Pinelands to the west.

This area is very special in historic significance as well. The many sugar-sand roads used in bygone days by those in the charcoal, cedar and bog iron industry are now used by hikers and bikers. It's not recommended for those unfamiliar with the area to attempt these roads by car, as they can be very sandy and the roads are unmarked. I've known a few locals who have driven for hours in their four-wheel-drive vehicles in an effort to get back to main roads. It's better to view the Forked River Mountains from nearby Jakes

The third level of the Nature Center at Jakes Branch County Park in Berkeley Township offers an astounding view of the Forked River Mountains, along with descriptive plates such as this, to describe the formation of these locally famous "mountains," of which the locals are so proud.

Branch County Park in Beachwood, where from the observation deck on the top level, you'll have a bird's-eye view of this mountain range of the Pines.

Great efforts are ongoing by the Forked River Mountain Coalition (FRMC) to preserve this land from development, as much of the land surrounding the mountains is in the designated Regional Growth Zone and is privately owned. The FRMC volunteers work to promote and preserve this region, including leading guided hikes—even one in search of the endangered and elusive Pine Barrens tree frog—canoe trips, cleanup days and more.

Popcorn Park Zoo Animal Rescue and Sanctuary

Many football fans may have heard of Princess the Camel, whose weekly football picks are better than most handicappers. You can meet Princess right here in the Pinelands at Popcorn Park Zoo in Lacey Township. Actually, she

This cougar lives a life of luxury at the Popcorn Park Zoo, located in the Pinelands of western Lacey Township. Both domestic and wild animals are rescued and given permanent homes here. The wild variety includes a number of cougars, lions, tigers, a camel, bears, deer and dozens of peacocks, just to name a few.

is one of many wild animals that have found forever homes at Popcorn Park; others include Bengal tigers, white-faced capuchins, macaques, horses, goats, emus, peacocks, tortoises, lizards, a wallaby, a lion and even a coatimundi. Popcorn Park Zoo, part of the American Humane Society, is a sanctuary for abandoned, injured, ill, exploited, abused or elderly wildlife, exotic and farm animals and birds. The animals at Popcorn Park have been rescued from circuses, zoos, farms or private owners who didn't realize the personal and financial responsibility of keeping a wild animal. Here at Popcorn Park, no animals are euthanized; they are well cared for by its many volunteers. The small admission fee charged helps defray the many expenses to house, feed and care for these animals. It's just a short drive on Lacey Road—only ten minutes from the Garden State Parkway.

Double Trouble State Park

Located on the eastern edge of the New Jersey Pine Barrens, with its main entrance on Pinewald Keswick Road, this park contains over eight thousand acres, about two hundred acres of which make up the historic district, which was once a working cranberry farm. Many buildings remain in this old company town, including workers' housing, a sawmill and the sorting and packinghouse with nearly intact equipment, which is open for guided tours in season. There are a few explanations for the name "Double Trouble." The most common is that the dam on the Cedar Creek washed out, causing

Cranberries ready for collection at Double Trouble State Forest in Berkeley Township. The old sorting house is in the background. While the cranberries are still growing in bogs, the land is no longer leased out for harvesting, so this scene is one that may not happen again at Double Trouble.

owner Thomas Potter to say, "Here's trouble!" When it washed out a second time in the same year, he called out, "Here's double trouble!"

The Cedar Creek, well known for canoeing, runs through Double Trouble and was the energy source for the sawmill, once used for the huge stands of cedars in the wetlands. This state-owned farm was a working farm leased to a local cranberry farmer until recently, when the farmer retired. Cranberries are still growing in the bogs, but the bogs may be left to be reclaimed by nature. Regardless, Double Trouble is an excellent example of a company town from years gone by. Free guided historical tours of the town are often available on weekends. A pleasant bonus is the 1.5-mile self-guided nature trail that loops around the bogs, providing informative and pastoral views of coastal pines, wetlands and cranberry bogs.

JAKES BRANCH COUNTY PARK

Just a short drive north on Double Trouble Road will take you to Jakes Branch County Park. Located just west of the Garden State Parkway in

A youngster gets a close-up look at insects of the Pinelands at one of the many displays inside the Nature Center at Jakes Branch County Park.

Beachwood, New Jersey, Jakes Branch is a recent addition to the Ocean County park system. The four-hundred-acre park offers soccer, baseball, tennis and basketball facilities and has a great playground for the kids. A picnic grove with grills and picnic tables is an inviting bonus. Only forty acres of this environmentally sensitive area were developed; the balance will remain in its natural state as preserved open space.

Best of all for those who want to gain a foundation of New Jersey's Pinelands is the wonderful nature center. Situated on a 77-foot-high hill, the 6,500-square-foot building offers a number of exhibits relevant to the Pine Barrens, and a live animal exhibit is in progress. There are plenty of hands-on exhibits for the young ones here, too. An avian observation area provides a great view to watch our feathered friends, and the 40-foot-tall outdoor observation deck, accessible through the nature center, offers a wonderful 360-degree view of the Pine Barrens. An elevator is available; take that up to the outdoor deck and then walk down to enjoy the exhibits as you descend. For hikers, a three-and-a-half-mile nature trail meanders through the preserved 360 acres of Pine Barrens. Jakes Branch also offers a number of weekend activities for both children and adults.

From Jakes Branch County Park, the township of Toms River is less than ten minutes north. While not within the official boundaries of the Pinelands, Toms River is the county seat of Ocean County and has a number of nice hotels and restaurants for visitors who want to extend their stay. A few miles east of Toms River is the resort area of Seaside Heights, with its amusement rides, wheels of chance and the many nightclubs popular with summertime visitors.

Chapter 7

Allaire State Park

As mentioned earlier, the New Jersey Pinelands is the delineated protection region set by the State of New Jersey and the Pinelands National Reserve as determined by federal authorities. The term "Pine Barrens" refers to an ecological region; this region extends farther north and south than do the state boundaries. In fact, an area of Middlesex County in the Helmetta area, an area roughly twelve miles by twelve miles, is what is known as the Spotswood Outlier and consists of typical Pine Barrens ecological characteristics.

Allaire State Park is located in Farmingdale, in Monmouth County. Although it is known best for the historic village, its 3,200 acres of Pine Barrens offer much more, including picnicking; hiking, biking and horseback riding trails; and boating on the Manasquan River. Camping is available for a small fee in tent and trailer sites, yurts and shelters and group campsites. The Manasquan River that flows through the park is stocked with trout annually, offering great opportunities for anglers, and provides a scenic and tranquil setting for canoeists; rentals are available. The Nature Interpretive Center, open seasonally, helps guide visitors to the natural areas of the park, where over two hundred species of wildflowers, trees and shrubs grow in their native habitat.

Historic Allaire Village

Once known as the Howell Works, Allaire Village was an industrial village that produced bog iron, as did so many villages of the late eighteenth and early nineteenth centuries. Today, buildings include a general store; a manager's house constructed in 1750, making it the oldest building in the village; a foreman's cottage, the oldest brick building here; a blacksmith shop; a carpenter's shop; a church; and the Allaire mansion.

One of the two remaining brick row houses once used to house the workers of Allaire is now a visitors' center and museum. There are a number of bog iron industry exhibits, information and artifacts about the Howell Works and James P. Allaire, who moved to this town in 1832 with hopes of providing his ailing wife, Frances, with the fresh country air of Monmouth County. The visitors' center and museum are open daily Memorial Day through Labor Day; call for off-season hours.

The Allaire General Store is a favorite among visitors. Browsing in this largest building of Allaire is akin to taking a trip back in time. You'll find handmade soap, beeswax candles, pottery, tinware, ironware, glassware, old-fashioned candy, books, souvenirs and more ever-changing gifts and household items. You're sure to find something here that you can't live without. Be sure to call ahead for hours.

If all those goodies in the general store weren't enough to satisfy, try the Howell Works Bakery. Here you can purchase freshly baked items, such as breads and flat cakes, and assorted beverages. You'll also be able to peruse a collection of early 1800s baking items.

A large variety of events is held at the village, such as craft shows, flea markets, Civil War encampments and the popular interpretive programs depicting life during the eighteenth and nineteenth centuries at the village. Activities such as cooking, household chores, militia drills, gardening, dye making and soap making are demonstrated. These interesting programs are usually available on weekend days from June through November.

Pine Creek Railroad

What youngster doesn't get a thrill from a ride on a train? Some of those youngsters grew up to run the Pine Creek Railroad, located within Allaire State Park, one of the oldest continually operating narrow-gauge steam preservation railway exhibits in the United States. Run by the nonprofit New

Jersey Museum of Transportation, Inc., train rides through the park are available for a small fee. Weekend and daily schedules vary depending on the time of year. The museum has a number of railroad cars either being restored by volunteers or on display; a railroad station and other structures are also on site.

Part III

Central Region

The central region can be considered the heart of the Pinelands, as there is so much to see here. It covers all the area roughly from Routes 72 and 530 south to the Atlantic City Expressway. Here we'll find cranberry farms, blueberry farms, historic villages, ghost towns and, of course, Wharton State Forest and Historic Batsto Village, with lots of interesting stops in between.

CHAPTER 8

Southampton, Pemberton and Medford

PINELANDS PRESERVATION ALLIANCE

Route 206 in the western area of the Pinelands is a great starting point for those coming from the Philadelphia area to discover the central region of the Pinelands, and the Pinelands Preservation Alliance (PPA) headquarters is a great place to start. Located on Pemberton Road just west of Route 206 (and just a few hundred yards outside of the Pinelands), the headquarters of this nonprofit agency offers a great visitors' center, complete with maps, books and exhibits to help guide you around the Pines. There's almost always someone around to answer questions, too. The Bishop Farmstead is a lovely location. The big two-story red Louden barn to the rear of the main farmhouse is simply bucolic, and in season, the gardens are filled with flowering plants. The farmhouse, built in 1753, houses the visitors' center and provides office space for staff and volunteers. An additional building offers meeting space for classes and seminars.

The PPA is the Pinelands' watchdog organization: while there are some paid staffers here who work relentlessly to assure that the Pinelands are not abused by illegal activities, the many volunteers donate countless hours toward protecting and preserving the history, flora, fauna and many resources of the Pinelands. The PPA offers a number of educational presentations, popular speakers and book signings and an exciting variety of canoe and hiking trips. A favorite among residents of the Pine Barrens who want to plant

The Pinelands Preservation Alliance headquarters are on the Bishop Farmstead in Pemberton Township. This beautiful Louden barn on the site was built in 1932 from a kit; the home that houses the staff and volunteers was built in 1753 and offers brochures, maps, books for sale and an interpretive center.

in harmony with nature is the annual Earth Day Native Plant Sale, where trees, shrubs, wildflowers, vines, grasses and wetlands plants that grow well in the acidic soils of this region are offered for sale. Many of these beautiful plants—especially the flowering ones such as the butterfly milkweed, which attracts butterflies—sell out before noon, so get there early.

North Pemberton Railroad Museum

Flanked by New York City to the northeast and Philadelphia to the west, along with major seaports along the waterways, it's easy to understand why railroads were once commonplace throughout the Pinelands. Tracks crisscrossed the area during the heyday of trains, and stations of varying sizes were scattered throughout the region. Today, not much remains in many areas but skeletons of those tracks, but a visit to the North Pemberton Railroad Museum, located on Fort Dix Road in Pemberton, will help you visualize what it once looked like. The railroad station was built in 1892 by John S. Rogers of Moorestown, replacing the earlier frame station that had burned in November 1891. It was in active use until 1969, when the last direct rail service between Pemberton and Camden ended. Restoration was completed in March 1999, and now the station is on both the New Jersey and National Registers of Historic Sites. The Railroad Station Museum is filled with many historical artifacts related to the railroad, the cranberry and blueberry industry and regional history. The gift shop contains a variety of books on New Jersey state history, regional history, the Pinelands, nature and, of course, the railroad.

Woodford Cedar Run Wildlife Refuge

Tucked into the Pines of scenic Medford Township is a wildlife refuge that takes in almost four thousand injured, orphaned or displaced animals a year. The refuge, located on the edge of the Pinelands, was once the private home of Jim and Betty Woodford, who dedicated their lives to preserving the Pinelands and its inhabitants. In the 1950s, they built a home on a 185-acre tract of land on the beautiful Cedar Run Lake and eventually developed this refuge.

While the goal of the refuge is to rehabilitate all animals brought there and return them to the wild, sometimes it is not able to do so, in which case the refuge becomes these animals' permanent home. On average, over sixty native animal residents live at Cedar Run, all in a natural environment. You'll see bald eagles, hawks, owls, foxes, vultures and others in outdoor enclosures that resemble their native habitats. Kids will love the Slither on Inn Reptile Room, where assorted snakes and turtles are on display, located at the Nature Center. The center hosts a variety of educational programs for all ages and has several hands-on exhibits for the casual visitor. Trails also meander from wetlands to uplands, and the center features an Adopt a Wild One program, whereby you can adopt one of the refuge's wild animals for a year. This helps to pay for its food and medical expenses, which in some cases can be quite expensive. Many fundraisers are conducted throughout the year to help defray costs for this worthwhile cause.

Woodford Cedar Run Wildlife Refuge is located at 4 Sawmill Road in Medford; a small admission fee is charged.

DR. JAMES STILL, BLACK DOCTOR OF THE PINES

James Still was born in Indian Mills in 1812. The son of slaves, his parents moved here from Maryland and lived deep in the woods, away from their former owners. Although he tried to obtain a college degree in medicine, because of his race and lack of funds, he returned home instead. As a child, he had learned many herbal remedies from medicinal plants from the Lenni-Lenape, so he set forth to educate himself. In time, he became a well-known herbalist; people of all races came from miles around to be treated by the "black doctor" of the Pinelands. Whatever money he earned with his cures, he reinvested in herbal medicine books in order to become a better healer. Dr. Still's office at 206 Church Road in Medford was built in 1836. This was Still's residence before he built another larger Victorian home adjacent to it. That home was demolished in 1932, but the smaller office was purchased in 2006 by the New Jersey Department of Environmental Protection in order to save it and the surrounding land where Dr. Still's personal residence once stood from commercial development. Today, it is listed on the New Jersey and National Registers of Historic Places. Interior tours are not currently offered.

James Still's youngest brother, William, grew up to become a well-known African American abolitionist and writer. He is best known for his famous historical account *The Underground Railroad*. Published in 1872, it is still in print and contains a collection of accounts by slaves, as well as authentic tales of freedom.

In 1877, Dr. James Still wrote his autobiography, *Early Recollections and Life of Dr. James Still*. Dr. Still was said to have been one of the largest landowners in Medford when he died in 1882. He is buried in the graveyard of Jacob's Chapel in Mount Laurel. His son, James Still Jr., was the third African American to graduate from Harvard Medical School and did so with honors. Another son, Joseph, continued his father's herbal curing ways. Today, James Still's great-great-granddaughter Francine Still-Hicks, herself an artist and author, speaks to groups about both James and William Still and their profound impacts. It has been said that the Still family, which today numbers in the hundreds, is one of the most prominent black families in the state of New Jersey, and it is certainly understandable why that just may be so.

CHAPTER 9

Tabernacle and Shamong

Travel east from Route 532 in Medford and you'll arrive in the town of Tabernacle, just east of Route 206. Located in prime farming area, you'll notice the vast fields of crops as you near the center of this small but charming town.

It is generally believed that Tabernacle, incorporated in 1901, was named for the log cabin tabernacle built by the Reverend John Brainerd at the site of the Tabernacle Cemetery, which is located at the intersection of Route 532 and Carranza Road. Reverend Brainerd was a Presbyterian missionary whose goal was to convert the Lenni-Lenape to Christianity. Brotherton, New Jersey's first and only Indian reservation, located just south in what is now Shaming or Indian Mills, was run by Brainerd. He named it Brotherton, with hopes that the Europeans who had colonized North America and the Native Americans who had peacefully existed here for centuries could co-exist. Started in the mid-1700s, those few Native Americans who had survived on the Brotherton reservation left in the early nineteenth century when they received an invitation from the Oneida Indians of New York to "come and eat out of our dish."

Today, Tabernacle remains a rural town with little more than its farms and farm markets, a restaurant and a local deli where locals can get breakfast or lunch, a gallon of milk, bread, cold cuts or other necessities of life that otherwise aren't found for several miles around.

Insider's Tip: Visit Russo's Fruit and Vegetable Market in the center of town. Much of their produce is grown right in Tabernacle, including our famous Jersey tomatoes and Jersey corn. It's also a good place to get fresh blueberries in June and July and cranberries from October to frost. Locally bottled blueberry iced tea and peach cider are also for sale. One of Russo's specialties is its apple cider donuts, baked right on site—it's hard to eat just one! Diagonally across from Russo's is the Tabernacle Cemetery, and beyond that is Nixon's General Store, a great stop for a deli sandwich and assortment of daily specials.

Russo's Fruit and Vegetable Farm is a Tabernacle landmark, and owner Anthony Russo Sr. is usually on hand to say hello—when he's not out working the fields.

Indian Ann

Indian Ann Roberts, the "last of the Delawares," lived in the Tabernacle area. One of the Lenni-Lenape tribe, she was born Ann Ashatama in 1804 somewhere near Mount Holly. As an adult, Ann would regularly be seen walking between her home in Indian Mills and Vincentown or Medford selling berries and baskets. Ann was married twice and had a son who died in service during the Civil War. Ann is best known for her basketry; today, her rare baskets are worth thousands of dollars. Ann is buried in the Tabernacle Cemetery.

Emilio Carranza

On a stormy night in July 1928, young Captain Emilio Carranza, then only twenty-three years old, was returning from a goodwill flight to New York City to his home in Mexico when lightning apparently struck his plane. It went down deep in the Pine Barrens, southwest of Chatsworth, where Carranza's body was found the next day by locals and was held at

Above: The entrance to the Tabernacle Cemetery, where the legendary Indian Ann is buried, is located at the intersection of Carranza Road and Route 532 in Tabernacle.

Left: The Carranza Memorial was erected in honor of Mexican hero Emilio Carranza, whose plane went down deep in the Pinelands during a thunderstorm in 1928. This monument was paid for by the children of his homeland; the stone was quarried in Mexico and then shipped and assembled deep within Wharton State Forest, near the site of his plane crash, where each year in July a festival is held in his honor.

Buzby's General Store in Chatsworth until it could be transported by train to New York and then flown back to Mexico. Carranza was a Mexican hero, revered by children and adults alike. After hearing of Carranza's death, the heartbroken children of Mexico collected funds, peso by peso, until they had enough to purchase the stone for the beautiful twelve-foot memorial that stands in his honor today. The stone was quarried from his home state of Coahuila, Mexico, where it was sculpted into the monument and then disassembled and sent to New Jersey, where it stands today deep in the Pines. Each summer, on the Saturday closest to July 12, a memorial service is held to honor Captain Carranza. This touching memorial is located on Carranza Road in Wharton State Forest.

To see this beautiful memorial, turn south onto Carranza Road and continue for about six miles past the farmland and into Wharton State Forest. The memorial is located on the right side of the roadway, just after the small parking area.

Friendship

The ghost town of Friendship is located about four miles beyond Carranza Memorial, but the road becomes a sugar-sand road, so traveling to it is not recommended without a four-wheel-drive vehicle. The roadway can become very muddy after a rain, and some shoulders are made up of soft sugar sand. Friendship today consists of foundations from what was once a busy village with a cranberry packinghouse, school, store and several homes. The bogs have been reclaimed by nature, and today this area is a popular spot for nature photographers.

Valenzano Winery

Valenzano Winery's vineyards and spacious tasting room/banquet hall are hard to miss when heading south on Route 206. Wine tastings are offered here, and often on weekends, musicians will be on hand to entertain you while you sip this local wine. Try the cranberry wine for a nice treat—it comes in both red and white. There are a number of other wines with a local flair, including Old Indian Mills Blend and the ever-popular Jersey Devil Port. Each year in September, Valenzano hosts a two-day Wine Fest, which draws thousands of visitors to the vineyard.

Valenzano Winery, a lovely and spacious facility that includes a large banquet room, is located on Route 206 in Shamong. Weekends are frequently busy, with a variety of events that usually include food, music and, of course, tasting the "wines of the Pines."

INSIDER'S TIP: If you're getting hungry from all the Pinelands fresh air, you're in luck. Just north of Valenzano Winery on the west side of Route 206 in Shamong is one of those special little diners that, if you blink, you'll miss altogether. It's appropriately called Shamong Diner. Its owner/chef, Manny, proffers a delectable assortment of breakfast, lunch and dinner selections, but locals and visitors "in the know" flock here for the twenty-six flavors of delicious ice cream, too. Of course, it's very family-friendly.

Pic-a-Lilli Inn

A few miles south is a favorite stop for visitors and locals alike—the Pic-a-Lilli Inn. It's easy to spot the big red fire truck parked out front with a sign that reads, "Our wings are so hot, we had to get our own fire truck!" This is a legendary yet very friendly bar/restaurant that's been in the same family since the 1920s. Its wings are known all over the region, but all of the food is consistently very good. Residents and visitors of all ages gather here regularly; it's well worth a stop.

Inside, a warm, inviting atmosphere welcomes guests. During cold winter days, one dining room usually has a fire going in its large fireplace in the center of the room, while the dining room just off the bar has a big-screen television for group gatherings. The feature of this room is the wall mural that depicts Pic-a-Lilli Inn as it looked many years ago, when it was a luncheonette that also sold gas.

The Pic-a-Lilli Inn is almost as famous for this fire truck in front of the restaurant as it is for its wings. As the sign on the truck reads, "Our wings are so hot, we had to get our own fire truck!"

CHAPTER 10

Wharton State Forest

ATSION AND QUAKER BRIDGE ROAD

Just about a mile south of Pic-a-Lilli Inn is the western reach of Wharton State Forest, named after financier Joseph Wharton. In the late nineteenth century, Mr. Wharton purchased much of the land that is now owned and protected by the State of New Jersey, with the anticipation that he would be able to sell the pristine waters from the Kirkwood-Cohansey aquifer system to Philadelphia, making a huge profit in the process. The New Jersey legislature, however, caught wind of his plans and passed a law prohibiting the exportation of water across state lines. Probably as a result of Wharton's plan, the state also enacted the New Jersey Forest Service in 1905 in order to protect its natural resources. In 1954, the State of New Jersey purchased the Wharton tract, and today it consists of over 100,000 acres, the majority of which are wooded. It also is home to some amazing historical sites, such as Atsion and Batsto, that are definitely worth a visit. Some of these places are discussed here, but entire books have been written about the towns, both past and present, that are located within Wharton's boundaries. Indeed, it's been said that there are more ghost towns in the Pinelands than in the entire West, and many of them are located right within Wharton.

Atsion is located in Shamong Township but within Wharton State Forest. During the peak of the iron industry in the Pinelands during the late eighteenth and early nineteenth centuries, about seven hundred people lived in Atsion. Even after the iron era ended, a paper mill, a cotton mill and a cranberry packinghouse were in operation here. Now, not much remains except the mansion, which is clearly visible from the roadway, the remains of an old schoolhouse, a few other buildings and some foundations. The church built by Ironmaster Samuel Richards in 1828 for the residents is still standing and is still in use today.

The Atsion Mansion is an imposing, salmon-colored building located on the east side of Route 206. Built in 1826 as a summer home for Richards, the mansion has recently been restored, and occasional tours of the interior are offered during summer months.

Atsion is located along Route 206 at Quaker Bridge Road, a hard-packed sugar-sand road, so named for the Quakers who in 1772 built a bridge over the Batsto River in order to attend the annual meetings in Tuckerton. This road was an important stage road connecting Philadelphia to Tuckerton, and a stage tavern was located just east of the bridge in the 1800s as a stopover for tired travelers.

Atsion Lake, on the western side of Route 206, offers a sandy beach for swimming in the clear (although slightly orange from iron oxide) waters and

The old schoolhouse at Atsion in Wharton State Forest is located on Quaker Bridge Road just beyond the mansion.

Above: The mansion at Atsion, located on Route 206 just south of Shamong, is within the Wharton State Forest. It was refurbished recently. The grounds are open to the public, but the mansion is not, although tours of the interior are occasionally offered.

Below: Quaker Bridge crosses the Batsto River deep in Wharton State Forest. The bridge was originally constructed by the Quakers in 1772 so that they could travel to the annual meetings in Tuckerton.

INSIDER'S TIP: One of the many legendary creatures of the Pines resided (and perhaps still does) near Quaker Bridge. The story goes that on a stormy night, a stage filled with travelers approached the bridge when out of nowhere, a big white buck appeared and blocked its way. The stage driver pulled his horses to a stop and dismounted in order to scare the buck away. Upon approaching, the buck did run, but the driver stared at the bridge in horror—the rains had washed it out! So if you happen to venture the four miles to Quaker Bridge, deep in the Pine Forest, keep an eye out for that big white buck.

a variety of camping facilities, including fifty tent and trailer sites with fire rings and picnic tables and a number of rustic cabins set along the north side of the lake. Showers, toilets and drinking water are all within walking distance of the sites. The campsite and park headquarters are open April 1 through October 31 each year.

BATSTO HISTORIC VILLAGE

If you visit no other historic village during your tour of the Pinelands, please visit Batsto. It's located on Route 542, which you can reach from Route 206 and Middle Road. Just look for the signs on the east side of the road, about four miles south of Atsion. As you reach Route 542, take note of the acres upon acres of blueberry bushes—you are now in blueberry country! These bushes are almost as pretty in winter as they are when they're loaded with berries in July. In winter, their branches are bright red in color and stand out nicely against the white sugar sand and snow. More about blueberries later, but you will pass a few farms along the way that do offer blueberries for retail sale, as well as wholesale. One of them is Mill Rock Blueberry Farm, where in late June through July, you will see a JERSEY FRESH sign over the barn entrance where pint boxes of blueberries are located. They can't get much fresher than this!

As you reenter Wharton State Forest near Batsto, the acres of blueberry farms will be overtaken by stands of pines and cedars. You are approaching historic Batsto Village. Batsto's history is fascinating. Its story began in the

A case of Jersey blueberries, arguably the best there are in the world, just packed and ready to eat.

mid-1700s as one of the first bog iron furnaces, built by Charles Read of Burlington, New Jersey. Bog ore was harvested from the lake that had been formed as a result of damming the Mullica River at the lumber mill. Through intense heat from the furnace, it was transformed into pig iron, so called because the molten iron ran into a form with lines of bars that resembled piglets suckling from their mother. This pig iron was then made into a variety of items, including, during the Revolutionary War, cannons, munitions, cap kettles and iron fittings. Of course, this made Batsto a target for the British, but the Mullica River, between the tricky tides and the privateers, proved too difficult for them to navigate.

In 1784, Batsto was acquired by the Richards family and for almost one hundred years was run by one of the Richardses. In the mid-1800s, iron production came to a halt, but not before the Richardses started to make glass for windows and streetlights, which lasted about twenty years.

A fire in 1874 destroyed much of the village, but the mansion and several other buildings are still standing today. The village was purchased by Millionaire Joseph Wharton, who purchased more land, increasing its size to ninety-six thousand acres.

The best way to learn Batsto's rich history is to head right to the visitors' center, located just off the main parking area. Be sure to allow time to stroll through the small museum, which is packed with artifacts from Batsto, including clothing, iron and glass products, a diorama of the town's layout and a timeline to put its historical changes into perspective. Once you've gotten an idea of the town's layout, grab a Cell Phone Audio Tour card

The gristmill at Historic Batsto Village is an attractive building, often seen in photographs and paintings. Inside the building are the huge wheels that once ground the various grains into flour.

and take off for the village, located just behind the visitors' center. With this handy guide, you'll be able to listen as you walk by the mansion, gristmill, icehouse, piggery, general store and other buildings that compose the restored village. Don't forget to walk to the sawmill, perhaps the most scenic location of Batsto, located just across from the beautiful Batsto Lake, a favorite for boaters and fishermen alike.

Batsto Post Office is one of four of the United States' oldest post offices currently in operation, and since it is a historical structure, it was never assigned a zip code. A visitors' center staff member will hand-cancel a postcard or envelope for you, and you'll see that no code is included in that stamp.

Guided tours of the mansion's decorated interior are available for a nominal fee, but days and hours vary. It's best to contact the Batsto Visitors' Center ahead of time if you would like to take this tour.

Its fascinating history is but one part of Batsto, however. There are several nature trails of varying length, including part of the Batona Trail, that run

Above: The museum in the visitors' center of Historic Batsto Village offers a lot of information, both historical and environmental, all in a well-designed layout, along with lots of fascinating artifacts from days gone by.

Below: The regal mansion is a major feature at Historic Batsto Village. Guided tours are available on selected days.

Insider's Tip: Make it a weekend getaway! On the third Sunday of October, Historic Batsto Village hosts its annual Country Living Fair, when the village comes alive with crafters, exhibits, music, old-time machinery and autos, antiques, quilting, food and lots more. This is held the same weekend as the annual Chatsworth Cranberry Festival, located about a half hour away. Nearby Hammonton has a few nice hotels, and of course, camping is available throughout the area.

through the Batsto region. They range in length from 1.0 mile to 9.5 miles, but my favorite is the Blue Trail. Hike it and you can claim you've hiked the Batona Trail, since they share a short path. This is also a good trail for spotting spring wildflowers, both upland and along the Batsto Lake. A brochure with maps of all Wharton trails is available at the visitors' center. Naturalist-guided hikes are available occasionally; give a call to the nature center or visitors' center to see what's coming up.

Once you've toured the farm and the workers' houses, you can either walk or drive to the Pleasant Mills Methodist Church, where Jesse Richards, one of Batsto's most beloved ironmasters, is buried along with his family. The original church was built in 1763 but was replaced in 1808 with the building that still stands today. Located just west of Batsto's workers' homes, a unique feature of this cemetery is that it is the only one in which iron grave markers are used. This church is still standing, and weekly services are still held here.

A Roman Catholic church was built nearby, along the Mullica River on Pleasant Mills Road. Jesse Richards donated this land for the church so his Catholic workers would have a place to worship. It was the first Catholic church to be built in what is now Atlantic County, New Jersey. As the iron and glass industries declined, attendance dropped. The church was eventually boarded up and was destroyed by a forest fire in 1900. Several tombstones dating back to the early 1800s remain, some surrounded by iron fences. Each year in early summer, local residents gather for the Blessing of the Mullica, a simple yet touching event that usually includes readings and songs to honor the past, present and future of the beloved Mullica River and ends with a floral wreath being tossed into the waters to be gently carried out to sea by the tides.

Pirates to Privateers

The islands in the Mullica River, some of which can be seen just behind the St. Mary's Cemetery, are a great example of why pirates loved this mysterious river. Driving south for a few miles on Pleasant Mills Road toward Sweetwater, you'll be able to see the many twists and turns and small wooded islands in this section of the river, which is fed by the Batsto and then continues east, taking with it the Bass and Wading Rivers, as well as a number of estuaries, before emptying into the Great Bay some twenty miles to the east. Indeed, these rivers and the pirate goings-on before and during the Revolutionary period are as good as almost any pirate-themed movie set in the Caribbean. Today, the Mullica is a lazy river serving as a nautical playground for those fortunate enough to live on or near its banks.

Before the Revolution, pirates roamed the waters of the Jersey bays and rivers. The tales that followed as a result are many, to say the least, and several books have been written about these dastardly characters. Indeed, much secrecy and espionage took place within this remote area between Philadelphia and New York City, with the port of Tuckerton—once the "third port of entry" into the colonies—in the middle of the maelstrom. The Mullica River empties just south of Tuckerton, more specifically, in the Mystic Island section of Little Egg Harbor Township. It is even rumored that in the late 1600s, the colorful Captain Kidd buried a trunk of gold somewhere near the mouth of the Mullica River. Privateers waited in this area for the British ships carrying booty to get stuck on the many sand shoals as they entered the Great Bay heading toward the Mullica.

Take Pleasant Mills Road south for a few miles. Shortly after turning, the Pleasant Mills Paper Mill is located on the left. This building was supposedly constructed as a warehouse for the privateers and those smuggling goods pillaged from the British destined for the colonial troops in Trenton and Princeton. It later became a paper mill, producing up to a ton of butcher paper a day in the 1880s. It has also been used as a cotton mill, a wool-reclaiming mill and a theater. It is now listed on the National Register of Historic Places. Across the road is the Elijah Clark Mansion, a stately Georgian Colonial built in 1762 and the setting for the novel *Kate Aylesford: A Story of the Refugees*, first published in 1855 and, more recently, as *Kate Aylesford, Or the Heiress of Sweetwater*, by Charles J. Peterson. The main character of the novel, which takes place during the American Revolution, is Kate Aylesford, so the home is also known as the Kate Aylesford Mansion. Today, it is a private residence.

Continuing on this road, you will see some very scenic overlooks of the Mullica interspersed among lovely riverfront homes and estates. Try to imagine the river filled with pirate ships. During the Revolutionary War, the Continental Congress authorized seafaring pirates, formerly a motley group of water-borne thieves, to act as privateers. This made all the previously illegal acts of capturing ships perfectly legitimate—as long as they were British ships. The privateers were able to pillage the ships and then hide within the islands until the right time came to sell the various supplies, much needed by Washington's army. The supplies were then shipped to Trenton, Philadelphia or wherever they were needed, and the captain and crew received a previously agreed-upon monetary award. The secret the privateers knew was the location of the many sandbars in the river. The British didn't know about these sandbars, so they invariably got stuck on them during low tides, rendering them helpless to the privateers, who then looted and burned the ships.

Sweetwater Casino

Sweetwater Casino was a Pinelands landmark for decades. Set along the idyllic Mullica River, this restaurant (it was not a gambling casino) was *the* location for weddings, birthdays, anniversaries, reunions, holiday dinners and repasts for locals and visitors alike, all of whom felt great personal loss when lightning struck in the wee hours of June 30, 2008. The restaurant burned to the ground despite valiant efforts by so many brave firefighters

The Sweetwater Casino was not a traditional casino but a longtime restaurant on the banks of the Mullica River. Sadly, it burned to the ground in the wee hours of June 30, 2008, but summertime visitors can still enjoy the beautiful sunsets on weekends at its Riverdeck.

and rescue squads. Fortunately, there were no injuries, but the loss was felt by thousands of patrons, family and friends. All that is left of Sweetwater are photographs and memories.

Today, the Sweetwater Riverdeck is open on weekends from May through October. This is a gorgeous place to watch the spectacular summer sunset over the Mullica River. You can still arrive by either car or boat. The ambience is still there, and the restaurant will never be forgotten.

Chapter II
Cranberry Country

Continue your drive while enjoying the scenery, and follow the signs through Weekstown to Route 563. A famous landmark of the region is Renault Winery, reached by traveling south on Route 563 to Moss Mill Road.

Renault Winery

Established in 1864, Renault Winery, with its handsome buildings, grounds and surrounding vineyards, is one of the oldest continually operating wineries in the United States. It was able to continue through Prohibition by making "medicinal cures." Tours are run here daily for a nominal fee. Tours begin in the beautiful Fountain Room and then head to the Antique Glass Museum with its interesting champagne and wine glass collection. You'll see the collection of old winemaking equipment and then visit the pressing room, where wines are made, and the wine cellar, where the casks of wine age. Tasting is available after the tour.

Renault's gourmet restaurant serves seven-course meals with two wine samplings and seasonal seafood buffets. Across the road is Renault's Tuscany House Hotel, which is also home to Joseph's, a very good restaurant with a Mediterranean flair, for breakfast, lunch and dinner. Also on site is the Vineyard Golf at Renault, a 7,200-yard championship golf course surrounded by vineyards, which is open to the public.

Head back to Route 563 north. Be sure to take in the beauty of the river as you cross the Mullica into Green Bank. A quick right turn onto River Road after crossing the bridge takes you right along the river for a short distance. This road, with its pretty homes and riverside docks, is reminiscent of bygone days in a sleepy river town. Turning left on River Road will take you past the historic Washington Township Municipal Building, also known as Shepherd's Hall, built in 1903.

Return to Route 563 and follow it north. As you continue north, be on the lookout for those telltale pink trail markers. The Batona Trail crosses the roadway here and then winds its way to its terminus at Bass River State Forest. Another interesting feature along this road is the Wading River, very popular with canoeists and kayakers. If you look carefully, you'll see a drop-off/pickup point on the east side of the roadway beside the bridge that crosses the river. Even on the hottest weekends of summer, one can paddle this quiet river without seeing another boater, but you certainly will see lots of interesting flowers, an occasional turtle sunning himself on a rock and possibly other innocent critters enjoying the forest. There are a number of canoe/kayak liveries in the area; you will pass Micks Pinelands Canoe and Kayak Rental as you travel north. Micks offers rentals for anywhere from two hours to overnight, with wilderness camping at a site adjacent to the river.

The forest will soon open up to large fields containing depressed areas surrounded by dykes. These are cranberry bogs. New Jersey consistently ranks among the top three states in the country in its cranberry production, behind only Wisconsin and Massachusetts, and the majority of those cranberries come from right here in the Pine Barrens. The cranberry was originally called a "craneberry" because the colonists thought this flower looked like the head of a Sandhill crane.

INSIDER'S TIP: The Green Bank Tavern is located at the corner of Routes 542 and 563. For years, this small, quaint bar has been known for its delicious chili, and it is a popular stop for motorcyclists out to enjoy the serenity of the Pines. The Lower Bank Tavern, another spot with good food, is just a few miles east on Route 542. Lower Bank Tavern offers a nice selection of food, and kids are welcome in the dining area. Owner Billy is also the chef and makes several dishes from scratch daily. Try the prime rib.

Depending on the time of year, these bogs will look very different. In the winter, the bogs are flooded to protect the vines from hard frost; in the spring, the bogs are green, followed in early summer by the cranberry flowers, which are a pinkish-white. Of course, harvest season is the most beautiful time of year to see these bogs, when they have been flooded, the berries have been harvested and they're floating on the water, ready for collection.

Contrary to popular belief, cranberries do not grow under water. They are vines that thrive in the acidic soil of New Jersey's Pinelands. Today, there are many varieties of cranberries. Scientists and farmers are working together to develop a plant that is resistant to the variety of weather conditions that can result in rot or fungus diseases. This research is important because fewer fungicides will be needed, which is ultimately good for consumers.

When a bog is ready to harvest, it will be filled with water from a nearby reservoir. Once filled, workers harvest the berries with a machine that looks a bit like a sideways eggbeater. This harvester pulls the berries off the vine with minimal damage.

The cranberries have four air-filled chambers, so they float right to the surface. Booms, much like those used to contain oil spills, are placed

A cranberry farmer stands knee-deep in the bog, waiting to coax the red harvest toward the collection area.

The actual harvesting of cranberries is accomplished with machines much like sideways eggbeaters. Once the bogs are flooded, these machines whisk the berries off the vines, after which they float to the surface and await collection.

around the perimeter of the bogs, and the cranberries are slowly drawn toward a vacuum-type machine that transports them through a cleaning conveyor and then to the trucks that take them for further processing. This procedure is called a wet harvest and is relatively new, having begun in the 1960s. Prior to that, the berries were dry-harvested, first by hand with cranberry scoops—a tedious, backbreaking job—and then with mechanical harvesters.

Cranberries are still dry-harvested today at some farms; these berries are usually sold at grocery stores and local farm markets and account for about 10 percent of the total harvest. Berries must be totally dry when harvested or else they will rot. Today, mechanical pickers are pushed through the vines, but until 1947, when the mechanical harvester was designed, the picking was done by hand with a cranberry scoop, a very time-consuming process.

The wet-harvested cranberries are used for juice, cranberry sauce and other cranberry products. Most cranberry farmers in this area belong to the Ocean Spray cooperative and truck their berries to a receiving

INSIDER'S TIP: If you're visiting during the cranberry harvest, keep in mind that these are privately owned commercial farms. Heavy machinery and tractor trailers go in and out of the farm all day long, so pick a safe place to park, out of the way of any roadways. It is ***not*** okay to pull into the farm without permission. Also, these farms cannot sell any cranberries to the public, as they all go to the Ocean Spray packing plant. If you want to purchase local cranberries, go to one of the local farm markets. One of these is Headley Farm Market on Route 9 in West Creek. You're not likely to get cranberries much fresher than from this family-owned and run shop.

station just up the road from the farms on Route 563. In season—late September through October—big tractor trailers loaded to the brim with berries can be seen up and down the road all day long.

The two farms located on Route 563 are Pine Island Farm, owned by the Haines family and the largest in the state, and, to the north, Lee Brothers Cranberry Farm. Many vines on these farms are fifty to seventy-five years old. The Lee family has been farming for five generations.

FRANKLIN PARKER PRESERVE

In 2003, the New Jersey Conservation Foundation purchased 9,400 acres from its former owner, who decided he wanted the land protected forever as a nature preserve. Today, it is open to the public, with over twenty miles of foot trails through uplands and wetlands that provide critical habitat to over fifty varieties of rare, endangered or threatened species of plants and animals. One entrance can be found north of the cranberry farms on Route 563; a second entrance can be found on Route 532 just west of Chatsworth. Both are marked with the New Jersey Conservation Foundation's prominent green sign.

Chatsworth and Buzby's Chatsworth General Store

Once you've had your fill of cranberries, head to the town of Chatsworth, lovingly called the "capital of the Pines" and located within Woodland Township. The beautifully restored Buzby's Chatsworth General Store is located in the center of this small village whose population is under one thousand. Buzby's is currently operating as a gift and book shop; hours vary, so it's wise to call ahead before you visit. If you are in town when the shop is open, it's well worth a stop to see the beautiful items on display, edible and otherwise. Also, the current book selection has a wide variety of books written about the Pinelands. Another favorite purchase is the Bog Beans, chocolate-covered cranberries.

Buzby's has a history that is vital to the Pinelands of today. Built in 1865, it was once a gathering place for locals who would sit on the porch and discuss the week's events in the Pines. A book that generally attributed to saving the Pine Barrens was written by John McPhee and entitled simply *The Pine Barrens*, first published in 1968. McPhee referred often to Buzby's, which was then an actual general store and gas station and where McPhee got

Buzby's Chatsworth General Store may well be the most recognized name in the Pinelands. This small, authentically restored building in Chatsworth, the "capital of the Pines," dates back to 1865 and is presently operated as a gift shop and bookstore. It is on the New Jersey and National Registers of Historic Places.

much of the information about the special place of which he was writing. Governor Brendon T. Byrne (after whom Lebanon State Forest was renamed) read McPhee's book and enacted statutes to establish what was to eventually become the New Jersey Pinelands Commission in order to preserve the land and the seventeen-trillion-gallon aquifer lying beneath it.

In the late 1990s, R. Marilyn Schmidt purchased the property, which had fallen into disrepair and sold at a sheriff's sale. Ms. Schmidt enlisted the services of master carpenter Albert Morrison and restored this historic building back to its original glory. It's now listed on the National Register of Historic Places.

Just across the street from Buzby's is Hot Diggity Dog, a popular sidewalk stand for a tasty hot dog or other quick snack and beverage. Just north of the stand is the historic White Horse Inn. This inn was painstakingly renovated by the Chatsworth Historical Society and is now open for tours, although it's recommended you call ahead for hours. Proceeds from the annual Chatsworth Cranberry Festival have been applied to the continued renovation and maintenance of this building. The White Horse Inn was built in the mid-1800s and called the Shamong Inn. Many wealthy tourists traveling from New York stayed here. In fact, Chatsworth at one time was the social spot for such millionaires as the Astors, Goulds, Abercrombies and others. A luxurious winter resort was built on nearby Chatsworth Lake, appropriately called the Chatsworth Club. This lake is located on Route 532 just west of town. During this time, Italian Prince Ruspoli, who was an attaché to the Italian Embassy, and his wife fell in love with the area and built a home dubbed the

The fire tower at Apple Pie Hill provides a panoramic view of the vastness of the New Jersey Pinelands.

Princess House near the lake as well. In its heyday, the Chatsworth Club had over six hundred members from Philadelphia and New York City, but eventually, interest waned, and the beautiful English Tudor mansion fell into disrepair. The prince and his wife returned to Italy. Nothing is left of either structure but a few scattered bricks, but the story has become part of Chatsworth's legend. Driving past Chatsworth Lake, the sandy shores on the far corner are but a subtle reminder of glorious days of the Gilded Age right here in the Pine Barrens.

Just a short drive west of Chatsworth Lake, Ringler Avenue is on the south side of the road. This will take you to the highest point in the Pinelands, Apple Pie Hill. The drive to the top of the hill is relatively easy, and the view from the fire tower, if you're so inclined to take the open stairway to the top, is spectacular. On a clear day, you may be able to see Atlantic City to the southeast and Philadelphia to the west, but more amazing is the view of the thousands of acres of pristine forest located in one of the most populated states in the country.

Chatsworth Cranberry Festival

Chatsworth is the location of what is one of the largest cranberry festivals in the country. For two days each October, hundreds of exhibitors and vendors line the streets and fields in celebration of the harvest. People throng here from all over the tri-state area and beyond to buy fresh cranberries, cranberry jam, jellies and salsas, cranberry breads and muffins, cranberry wine and an

The Chatsworth Cranberry Festival, one of the largest in the country, runs for two days during the third weekend of each October.

amazing assortment of artwork and crafts from regional artisans. A huge food court offers a huge variety of gastronomical delights, and entertainment is provided by a local band.

> Insider's Tip: This festival is enormous and parking is very scarce, although efforts have been made to provide additional space. Parking is permitted along Route 532 either side of Route 563, but if you don't want to walk a mile or more, get to the festival early—8:00 or 8:30 a.m.—for a decent spot. There are also private lots that offer parking scattered about town for a fee of five or ten dollars. The roads, especially Route 563, are all but gridlocked by midday, so another alternative is to go later in the afternoon, but keep in mind that some vendors are beginning to pack up by 3:00 or 4:00 p.m., especially on Sundays.

Warren Grove

From Chatsworth, Route 532 east will take you back to Route 72. Take it east, passing through the pygmy pine forest, to Route 539 south into Warren Grove, probably best known for its small diner, Lucille's Country Cooking. This longtime landmark is a regular stop for many locals, as well as those traveling to the shore from points north, who often make it a breakfast or lunch must-stop. Not fancy by any means (few places in the Pine Barrens are), the food is as its title states: country cooking. Of special note is the chili, but the pies may well be what bring visitors back again and again. It's hard to miss, since it's about the only business in this tiny hamlet.

There is one other interesting business you might want to see. It's called simply the Bog, and it is a huge aboveground bog filled with over six hundred carnivorous plants. Bill Smith, owner of the bog, humbly considers his creation the largest aboveground bog in America. Bill cultivates his own plants; he does not take them from the bogs of the Pinelands. Bill is an expert on these plants, as well as other rare species such as orchids, a number of endangered species of which grow in the Pinelands. In the event that carnivorous plants are something you might

This purple pitcher plant (*Sarracenia purpurea*) grown by "Bogman" Bill Smith is one of many that he has growing in his huge man-made aboveground bog in Warren Grove.

Blackened pines were visible to the horizon after the huge fire of 2007 that destroyed over seventeen thousand acres of Pinelands in southern Ocean County.

like to grow, Bill does sell them as well. The Bog is tucked away off Route 539 near Lucille's—look for the sign—but give Bill a call if you want a personal tour of his bog.

Continuing along Route 539 west for a few miles, you will enter the East Plains of the pygmy pine forest. This is the primary location of the huge forest fire of 2007 that burned over seventeen thousand acres of forest as a result of an errant bomb released at the nearby Warren Grove Bombing Range. In fact, you will drive right by Bombing Range Road in the pygmy pines, part of which is open to the public. Look closely at the tiny trees and you'll still see evidence of this huge fire.

Stay on Route 539 to return to the Garden State Parkway or, beyond that, Route 9, both of which run north–south along the Pinelands' eastern borders.

Part IV

The Central Coastal Corridor

The Atlantic coastal area is generally fairly populated, with the exception of those lands protected by federal, state or local government and several nonprofit agencies. Many towns straddle Route 9, the north–south corridor that runs from North Jersey to Cape May in the southern tip of the state. These towns, for the most part, date back to the colonial days, when Europeans chose to settle close to major waterways. Here, the Pinelands meet the bays, resulting in a happy merger of forest and shore. The barrier islands beyond the bays are summer playgrounds for children of all ages, but because of centuries of development as summer resorts, most are not part of the National Reserve, with the exception of Island Beach State Park, located across the inlet from Barnegat Lighthouse State Park. These long, narrow islands offer white sand beaches and clean ocean waters, lodging ranging from hotels to long-term oceanfront mansions and a plethora of dining and entertainment options.

Chapter 12

Stafford Township/ Manahawkin

First settled by colonists before 1700, the earliest industries in Stafford Township were sawmills and gristmills. Cedars, which thrive in the low-lying areas of the coast, provided lumber. The historical society headquarters is located in the Old Stone Store located just off Route 9 across from Manahawkin Lake. It's part of Heritage Park, which includes the old Manahawkin Railroad Station—moved here in 1990 from its original location on Stafford Avenue—and a restored railroad passenger car. The Cultural Center is located in the historic Old Manahawkin Baptist Church, just north of the lake on Route 9. It is used for meetings and is a depository for artifacts relating to the area.

Stafford Township was once home to an iron forge, and cranberry farms dotted its landscape. In fact, an elementary school and street are named after a former cranberry plantation located at the headwaters of Manahawkin Lake. The farm was named Oxycocus (the scientific name for cranberries) by its owner, Nathaniel Holmes Bishop III, a successful author and cranberry farmer during the late nineteenth century. Manahawkin Lake now offers swimming and picnicking in season.

Today, Stafford Township is a thriving area, with a population topping twenty-six thousand. A large commercial area along Route 72, from the Garden State Parkway east to the causeway bridge to Long Beach Island, serves its residents, along with those of neighboring towns and summer visitors to the shore. In part due to its proximity to this popular seashore resort, Stafford Township's population soared during the late 1990s. It is

Insider's Tip: Long a local tradition, the Manahawkin Flea Market is open every Friday, Saturday and Sunday. Located on East Bay Avenue about one and a half miles east of Route 9, this is a great spot to get some of the best freshly picked Jersey corn and tomatoes along the coast, and the prices are great. Landscaping plants, both annuals and perennials; seashore-geared gifts; jewelry; an Italian bakery; a cheese shop; and lots more, both indoors and out, are open early for those hitting the ocean for a day in the sun. The indoor shops are open seven days a week; a farmers' market is offered on Fridays during the summer.

For a delicious lunch when you're done, head a mile east to Mud City Crab House. Named after the small development on Mallard Island just across the street that is fondly called Mud City by locals, this restaurant offers a delectable assortment of fresh seafood. Open seasonally (call for hours), this casual restaurant has a huge following, and for good reason. I happen to love the seafood bisque and steamed Ipswich clams, but everything I've ordered here is just wonderful.

composed of many neighborhoods, including Manahawkin, Ocean Acres, Beach Haven West, Cedar Run, Mallard Island and others, each with its own personality.

Just a few miles south of Route 72, off Route 9 via Cedar Lane, is the Stafford Forge Wildlife Management Area. This 11,500-acre reserve was once the site of Stafford Forge, founded in 1797 by John Lippincott, and was also once the Stafford Cranberry Plantation Bog. Today, its scenic lake-like areas make it a great spot for hiking or just enjoying nature.

Continuing south to Tuckerton, stop into Headley Farm Market on Route 9 in West Creek for fresh produce in season and, in the fall, freshly dry-harvested cranberries right from the Headley bogs about a mile away. There aren't too many places in the area where you can get cranberries as fresh as these. This small but chock-full shop is located between Sleepy Hollow Restaurant and Pine Barrens Antiques on the west side of Route 9.

Chapter 13
Tuckerton

Continue south along Route 9 for about eight miles and you'll arrive in Tuckerton. This town was once considered the "third port of entry" because of its easy access from Little Egg Harbor Bay, and today, it still retains a nautical feel. Needless to say, there is much fascinating and colorful history in this quaint, picturesque town that is unknown to many visitors to the Jersey Shore. Much of the town has a Victorian flair, and many of the homes date back to this period. The small shopping district is also in keeping with the Victorian theme. Tuckerton was once the destination of stagecoaches coming via the Tuckerton Stage Road from Philadelphia, and Quakers traveled via Quaker Bridge Road to attend the annual meetings here. The Tuckerton Railroad was built in 1872, bringing even more visitors to the area.

Ocean County Decoy and Gunning Show

Tip Seaman County Park is located on Route 9 in Tuckerton, on the southern shore of Lake Pohatcong. This twenty-two-acre park was named after Stanley "Tip" Seaman, a well-known area personality and county freeholder in the 1970s. It is probably best known for the annual Ocean County Decoy and Gunning Show, named as one of the top one hundred events in the country. This two-day event is held the last weekend of September and is shared with Tuckerton Seaport, located just across Route 9 from Tip Seaman Park.

These working decoys were winners at the Ocean County Decoy and Gunning Show.

Vendors and exhibitors come from all over the East Coast to display their works of art and wares. Over five hundred vendors and exhibitors under two huge tents and throughout the park offer hunting and fishing supplies and clothing, carving materials, decoys, antiques, kayaks, canoes, boating supplies, dog supplies and even puppies. Competitions are held for artistic and working decoys, gunning boats, duck and goose calling, skeet shooting, archery, water retrieving (dogs), artwork and more. A large variety of food is available. Admission is free, and shuttle buses are available from the parking areas. No wonder it's one of the largest shows of this type!

TUCKERTON SEAPORT

Certainly a popular tourist feature in Tuckerton is the beloved Tuckerton Seaport. Sprung from a dream of local residents who made it a reality through blood, sweat and tears, this wonderful working maritime village has a number of historic and re-created buildings that give the visitor a look at the way of life of the Bayman. The Tuckerton Yacht Club, a re-created building, houses the huge gift shop and is the starting point of the village tour. From here, access to all the exhibits and displays and information about current programs, classes, demonstrations and even boat rides can be found.

On the upper level, the Jacques Cousteau National Estuarine Research Reserve has on display a state-of-the-art "Life on the Edge" exhibit, which introduces visitors to the diversity of the headwaters of the Mullica River. The lower lever, which leads to the boardwalk, is home to a variety of fascinating exhibits. The three-quarter-mile boardwalk fringes Tuckerton Creek. Stops along the way might be a decoy carving shop, where expert carvers work and talk about their art; a sawmill; or parson's clam and oyster house, where on some days, local Baymen might be giving classes on how to shuck these tricky bivalves. At the Seaport, you'll find out why Tuckerton flourished as "Clam Town" and learn the intricacies of clamming the traditional way: tonging, treading and raking. The oyster house also features the fascinating history of New Jersey's oyster industry, from methods of catching shellfish to shipping them to market. Also along the boardwalk is the re-creation of Perrine Boat Works (the original, although long closed and boarded up, is still standing in Barnegat), a functional boat works with exhibits on the history of traditional boat building. It includes vintage and newly constructed Barnegat Bay sneakboxes and garveys. If you're lucky, a traditional artist will be on site at one or all of these exhibits, demonstrating his/her craft, but it's best to call for scheduled times.

George Ross, a master decoy carver for many decades, often carves in front of audiences at Tuckerton Seaport or here at the annual Waterfowling and Family Fun Day at the Natural Resource Education Foundation at the Lighthouse Center in Waretown.

Tuckerton Seaport's flagship is this re-creation of Tucker's Island Lighthouse, located at the head of Tuckerton Creek. A number of exhibits are housed inside the lighthouse, including a photo display of the original lighthouse falling into the bay.

The highlight of Tuckerton Seaport is the re-created Tucker's Island Lighthouse, built in 2000. The lighthouse features exhibits on the history of New Jersey lighthouses, navigation, the U.S. Life Saving Service, pirates, whaling and life at what is claimed to be the first seaside resort along our coast. Tucker's Island, or Sea Haven, was a barrier island located just south of Long Beach Island. The first lighthouse was built in 1848, followed by a second in 1865. Weather, time and tides took their toll, and around 1900, a series of storms and hurricanes washed away much of the sand composing Tucker's Island. Over time, the lighthouse and other buildings were abandoned, and on October 12, 1927, Tucker's Lighthouse literally toppled into the water. A sequence of photos documenting this event adorns the walls of the "new" Tucker's Lighthouse to astound the many visitors to Tuckerton Seaport.

Tuckerton Seaport holds a number of events throughout the year. The Red Wine and Blues Festival features local wineries offering their products, with blues music as a backdrop. The annual Baymen's Seafood and Music

Festival serves up clams, crabs, scallops and shrimp. There is also Haunted Seaport at Halloween and Christkindlmart, a two-day event that offers up holiday crafts and gifts under huge heated tents, carolers, mulled cider, roasted chestnuts, children's rides and other special surprises to make for a special old-fashioned Christmas spirit.

Seven Bridges Road

Just past Tuckerton Seaport on the left is Great Bay Boulevard. The Tuckerton Center of the Jacques Cousteau National Estuarine Research Reserve (JCNERR) is located about a quarter mile down on the right. The JCNERR is composed of twenty-seven reserves around the country developed to protect estuaries where rivers meet the sea. The Pinelands is privileged to have one right here, working to protect the Mullica-Great Bay ecosystem. Run through the Tuckerton Center, the base for education and outreach programs offered by the reserve. Administered by Rutgers, the State University of New Jersey, the Tuckerton Center includes a classroom equipped with video conferencing, Internet-capable computer workstations, a library of K–12 curriculum materials and a sixteen-bed dormitory. Although the center is designed to primarily serve adult learners such as K–12 teachers and coastal decision-makers, programs for families, senior citizens and students are also held here and at the Tuckerton Seaport. The Seaport also hosts the JCNERR's beautiful exhibit, "Life on the Edge."

Continue on Great Bay Boulevard for a few miles and you'll be rewarded with excellent views of the coastal wetlands. Nicknamed "Seven Bridges Road," this roadway really does have seven bridges of varying heights and lengths. The most interesting may be the one with the signal to regulate traffic, as the bridge has only one lane. At the end of the road is another private marine research facility run by Rutgers and a trail that runs through brush (watch out for all the poison ivy!) to the bay, great for watching nature and the boats on the bay.

From here, you will also be able to see the remains of the old fish factory on Crab Island, also known as Fish Island. Built in 1930, it was a processing plant for menhaden, also called bunker, an oily, smelly fish. Menhaden were once plentiful in the surrounding waters and were processed mostly for fertilizer and animal feed. Workers arrived at the island via boats from docks off Seven Bridges Road. The stench during the processing could be smelled for miles around, and it took the workers several washings to be clean of it. The factory eventually closed when menhaden supplies diminished. It was eventually given to the state for preservation. A fire in 1982 severely damaged the building. It is forbidden to walk on the island, but boaters who can outsmart the biting flies and mosquitoes often fish for striped bass in the area.

The Tuckerton Wireless

Built in 1912, the Tuckerton Wireless that once stood in the Mystic Islands section of Little Egg Harbor Township was said to have been the most powerful transatlantic radio transmitter in America and, at 820 feet, the second largest in the world; only the Eiffel Tower was larger. Oddly enough, this tower was actually built by the German government in what was then a desolate area of South Jersey, allegedly without the knowledge of the U.S. government until it was almost completed. At the time, the United States was not involved in World War I. Once the tower was discovered, the transmissions were monitored to be sure messages were neutral. The Tuckerton Tower was used to communicate with an identical tower located in Germany, as well as with German ships and submarines. Of course, with secret codes, that was almost impossible; in fact, it is a strong theory that the message "Get Lucy" was transmitted as a signal for German submarines to attack the British passenger liner *Lusitania*. The United States entered World War I in 1917; at that time, it took over control of the tower. After the war, RCA ran the Tuckerton Tower until World War II, when the United States once again took over operations. The transmitter was demolished in 1955.

The Tuckerton Historical Society Building displays the base of the transmitter, the only remaining part known to be in existence today, in its front yard. Photos of the tower's demolition and lots more information are on display at the historical society. The twenty- by twenty-foot concrete anchors for the guy wires that once supported the transmitter are located in the Mystic Island section of Little Egg Harbor Township, reached via the aptly named Radio Road.

Chapter 14
Bass River to Oceanville

Bass River State Forest

Yet one more jewel in the New Jersey Pinelands necklace is the beautiful Bass River State Forest. Located on Stage Road just about ten minutes from Tuckerton, Bass River is made up of over twenty-seven thousand acres, much of it wilderness. The beautiful Lake Absegami, Native American for "little water," is a major feature of this forest and provides a majority of its recreation.

The sixty-seven-acre lake was constructed by members of the Civilian Conservation Corps (CCC), an organization created in 1933 during President Franklin D. Roosevelt's term in office in an effort to get men back to work during the Great Depression. Two hundred or more men worked here between 1933 and 1942. During that time, they built roads, trails, bridle paths, vehicular bridges, ponds, nature observatory shelters, fire towers, picnic areas, campsites and Lake Absegami. Today, their work is remembered on a self-guided trail with a memorial near the foundations of the CCC camp.

The Absegami Nature Area is composed of 128 acres around Lake Absegami, where you can take a self-guided half-mile walk through a wetland forest of cedars, maples and magnolias or choose from eight easy walking trails from a half-mile to 3.2 miles in length. The Batona Trail also ends here at Bass River, so it's a veritable hiker's dream. Add to that the sandy beach and clear lake waters at the beach complex and 176 tent and trailer sites.

BATTLE OF CHESTNUT NECK

About ten miles south of Tuckerton is Port Republic. The village of Chestnut Neck is located at the mouth of the Mullica River (once known as the Little Egg Harbor River). During the Revolutionary War, this area was a hotbed for privateers, who laid in wait for British ships to enter the Little Egg Harbor Bay. Over thirty-five ships were captured and their cargo sold.

In October 1778, the British invaded Chestnut Neck. Its defenders had no cannons or other artillery, so they could not protect the village or its contents and fled to the woods. The British destroyed ten vessels, two landings, three saltworks and ten buildings owned by Patriots. When General Casimir Pulaski of the Continental army arrived a few days later, the British, having already been informed of their arrival by a spy, proceeded to massacre the troops.

Much intrigue and possibly espionage is connected with this battle, and books are available that recount it in great detail. A statue dedicated on October 6, 1911, in honor of those killed is a touching tribute. The fifty-

A close-up of the lone Revolutionary soldier guarding the shores.

INSIDER'S TIP: If you're feeling hungry for some fresh seafood or a delicious burger about now, look for a sign for Mott's Creek Inn about two and a half miles south of Chestnut Neck on Route 9. Turn east and follow it to its end at Mott's Creek Inn. This place isn't fancy—in fact, it only has a few tables surrounding the bar with gorgeous views of the bay—but it's filled with friendly people and delicious food. My favorite is the Seafood Boat Bottoms—homemade potato skins filled with scallops, shrimp and crabmeat, baked with a three-cheese blend and topped with Old Bay seasoning, sour cream and chives. The Drunken Clams, local clams in a wonderful white wine sauce served with fresh Italian bread for dipping, come in a close second.

foot-tall statue, erected through the efforts of the General Lafayette Chapter of the Daughters of the Revolution, is that of a lone Minuteman facing east, still guarding the shores. The plaque reads: "In honor of the Brave Patriots of The Revolutionary War who defended their liberties and their homes in a battle fought near this site October 6, 1778."

SMITHVILLE VILLAGE

Continue south on Route 9 for about a mile and Smithville Village will be on the right. The Historic Smithville Inn has been feeding travelers since 1787. There are over fifty shops and eateries here, and the kids will love the mini-train, carousel and paddle boats on the lake. Two bed-and-breakfasts offer a variety of overnight accommodations.

Smithville Village is actually a "created" village. In the early 1950s, Fred and Ethel Noyes purchased an old run-down building and seven acres located on what is now Route 9. The building, which was built in the late eighteenth century, had been used as an inn in years past but needed much work. They completely refurbished it and opened it as a restaurant and then went on to purchase a number of historic buildings and move them to what is today called Towne of Historic Smithville Inn. When the Noyeses sold the developed "town" in 1974, it consisted of over 2,300 acres with several shops, inns and a hotel. The Noyeses then purchased another restaurant, which today is known as the Ram's Head Inn, an elegant restaurant in nearby Galloway.

EDWIN B. FORSYTHE NATIONAL WILDLIFE REFUGE

Just over a mile south on Route 9 is Great Creek Road, which goes to the main office and well-known Eight-Mile Road of the Forsythe Wildlife Refuge. Here, for a small fee, you can drive a hard-packed dirt road along the coastal wetlands. A visitor information center is located at the beginning of the drive and provides bird checklists, auto tour guides and refuge brochures, as well as recent wildlife sightings and other important information. Barrier-free restrooms are also available.

During the spring and fall migration, this place is teeming with birds taking a well-deserved break from their long journeys. Bald eagles, herons, terns, great egrets, falcons, ospreys and many other species can be seen here, offering amazing photo opportunities. Come winter, the huge flocks of snow geese are astonishing. Near sunset, they all take to the skies at once; often, thousands will all but obliterate the sun.

It's important to keep in mind that this is a refuge, and as such, the speed limit on this road is fifteen miles per hour; the wildlife must not be fed; and

The Edwin B. Forsythe Wildlife Refuge in Oceanville offers an eight-mile loop road into the open bay for viewing birds year-round. In addition, several overlooks are available, such as this one, where the impressive skyline of Atlantic City's casinos is visible in the distance.

the flora and fauna should not be disturbed. An amazing sight to see from this drive is the Atlantic City skyline just across the bay. It seems odd that two so extraordinarily different worlds can be so close.

A songbird hiking trail is located in the wooded area adjacent to a picnic area. Here, you're likely to spot a wide variety of upland wildlife species, including songbirds, woodcock, white-tailed deer and box turtles.

Noyes Museum of Art

From the Forsythe Wildlife Reserve compound, follow the signs to the Noyes Museum of Art. Opened in 1983, this striking building with the picturesque Lily Lake as its background is run in partnership with Stockton State College. It was a vision of Fred Noyes and his wife, Ethel, who passed away in 1979. Today, over two hundred of Fred Noyes's own paintings and those from his collection, as well as his extensive collection of decoys—one of the largest on the East Coast—are on exhibit at the museum, along with ever-changing exhibits of regional artists.

CHAPTER 15

The Jersey Devil

The Jersey Devil is alive and well in the New Jersey Pinelands! This ageless creature has been around for centuries and isn't likely to go anywhere soon; in fact, he is one of the most popular attractions. Books and poems have been written about him, sports teams have been named for him, songs have been sung about him, documentaries have been produced about him and television shows and even movies have been based on him. The Jersey Devil is one popular creature.

I include the Jersey Devil within the central coastal region because it seems he spends most of his time here. Legend has it that he was in fact born here, right in Leeds Point, just east of Smithville. As one version of the legend goes, around 1735, Mother Leeds, pregnant with her thirteenth child, experienced a painful delivery and at one point announced, "May the devil take this one!" At birth, the child was an average-looking baby who quickly transformed into the Jersey Devil, with horns atop his horse-like head, glowing red eyes, bat-like wings, talons on his hands, a body covered with both fur and feathers, the legs of a goat and the tail of a serpent. He grew before their eyes to over seven feet tall. Before he took off up the chimney (or out the window, depending on the version), he killed his mother, brothers, sisters and everyone else in the house.

To this day, the Jersey Devil roams the Pinelands and is even spotted from time to time, though his presence is more likely to be felt rather than seen. One of the Jersey Devil's best-known tirades was in 1909, when he allegedly terrorized towns and the countryside from Philadelphia

An interesting rendition of the Jersey Devil by local artist Susan Ramp.

through South Jersey. In some towns, dead chickens were found in the yards and strange hoof prints were found in the snow on the ground, on roofs and heading up trees, with the prints suddenly ending in the middle of a field or street. Visual reports were made of a flying animal with red glowing eyes, of trash being strewn about and, in one case, a woman's dog caught in its grasp. Witnesses included a police officer and even a man of the cloth. Since that time, reports have been made, though none so widespread as the 1909 outbreak.

If you happen to drive to Leeds Point via East Moss Mill Road or Leeds Point Road, you may come upon an old home that many believe is his birthplace, but this is not true. The Leeds home is long gone, and the location of its foundation can only be reached via a trail off a main road into the woods, one that I do not suggest you take. Those local residents who do know where this trail is will not speak of its location. It is also rumored that he spends a lot of time around Scott's Landing, a public small canoe and kayak launch located in Leeds Point, owned by the U.S. Fish and Wildlife Service and maintained by Forsythe Wildlife Refuge. Many people have told me of the strange feeling of another "presence" in these wooded wetlands adjacent to Forsythe Wildlife Refuge and other areas within the Pinelands. Someone once described to me what happened while she was hiking within Wharton State Forest near Batsto Lake. She experienced a sudden drop in temperature and a foul smell and then saw a shadowy figure in the distance. Her young child then ran up to her and told her that they must leave because "something bad is here." Believe or don't believe—it is up to you.

INSIDER'S TIP: If all that Jersey Devil hunting has whetted your appetite, you're in luck. Take Leed's Point Road or East Moss Mill Road to Oyster Creek Road and follow that to the end. You'll arrive at the Oyster Creek Inn, an amazing seafood restaurant. With its wind-worn cedar shakes, this restaurant is unimposing from the outside but offers up some delicious seafood meals, most of which are created with local catch. Oyster Creek Inn is known for its crab cakes, scallops, fresh sushi and sashimi tuna and variety of grilled fish, but steaks are excellent as well. Summertime weekends are usually busy, but it's well worth the wait. Sit outside on the deck, order one of the yummy appetizers—maybe some fresh oysters or clams on the half shell—and watch the spectacular sunset on the water. If you opt to stay indoors while you're waiting, stop at the bar and order up a Jersey Devil Cocktail.

Fresh scallops are but one of the specialties offered at Oyster Creek Inn in Leeds Point, home of the legendary Jersey Devil. The Jersey Devil Cocktail, a blend of brandy, cranberry juice and 7-UP, is on the bar menu.

The Leeds family is alive and well today in Galloway Township; if you're lucky, you might run into one of these lovely people. Several years ago, I had the pleasure of meeting the very charming Harry Leeds, longtime mayor of Galloway Township, who passed away in 2011. He told me definitively that he was an eleventh-generation Leeds, directly descended from Mother Leeds, and further that the Jersey Devil never killed anyone. With a twinkle in his eyes, he pointed to his forehead and said, "See those two little bumps there? I've got a bit of devil in me!" Leeds has told some people that he saw the Jersey Devil and described him as a "hideous creature," with his most distinguished feature his "piercing red eyes."

Of late, it seems as though the Jersey Devil is keeping a watchful eye on his domain. There have been more than a few rumors that those who disregard the sanctity of nature here in the Pinelands by littering the land, polluting the water or generally destroying it through misuse have had very unpleasant encounters with the Jersey Devil. It seems this irritates him quite a bit. It's not a good idea to irritate the Jersey Devil.

For those who dare to explore it, there is a Route 666 within the ecological Pine Barrens. Also called Bridgeton Avenue, it's located in Deerfield Township, just west of Vineland.

Part V

The Southern Pinelands Region

The southern region of New Jersey's Pinelands begins in northern Cape May County (the actual "cape" is not included), includes portions of Gloucester and Cumberland Counties and, for the purposes of this book, extends roughly to Route 30 in Atlantic and Camden Counties. Much of this area is rural; indeed, it's hard to believe, even for a Jersey girl like myself who has lived in the Pinelands for many, many years, that this rustic countryside is really New Jersey. Interspersed between pine oak forests and cedar-lined wetlands teeming with waterfowl are lush horse farms and hamlets; no chain-store restaurants or department stores interfere with the scenery or senses here. The occasional small pub or restaurant is far outnumbered by quaint old churches and community centers in this region, reminiscent of decades, perhaps even centuries, gone by. Time seems to have slowed down, especially in the Delaware Bay, or "Down Jersey," area. For example, if you stop into a small gift shop at the rear of a home, a loud beep alerts the owner that a customer has arrived, and only then does she walk back to the shop to be of help. This is the way of life in the southern Pinelands: peaceful, relaxed and free of the hustle and bustle of today's frenzied world. This is a New Jersey that few know exists, a far cry from the stereotypical cities of the North.

This area is also home to both the Cape May and Delsea regions of the New Jersey Coastal Heritage Trail; the Cape May National Wildlife Refuge, consisting of 11,500 acres; and a number of wildlife management areas.

The Delaware Bay has been an important source of seafood for centuries and still is. Tiny towns with names like Bivalve and Shell Pile dot the coast. Birders travel from many miles around to this region because of its location on the Delaware Bay, which is a major stopover for birds migrating via the Atlantic Flyway; in fact, the Delaware Bay shoreline has gained international recognition as a major shorebird staging area in North America, second only to the Copper River Delta in Alaska.

The southern Pinelands can be easily accessed via the New Jersey Parkway from the north or the Cape May–Lewes (Delaware) Ferry from the south. Lodging is varied here. There is everything from oceanfront resorts in the limelight of the glitz of Atlantic City's casinos to the boardwalk hotels of Wildwood, where the kids can get their fill of rides and arcades. You'll find quiet B&Bs in Cape May or quaint cottages in Cape May Point. Of course, camping is available at a number of private campgrounds throughout the Pinelands, as well as at state and local parks and forests, all within about a half hour of exploring this fascinating region.

Chapter 16

Mauricetown and the Maurice River

Before going any further, know that this town is pronounced "Morristown," as is the river of the same name. It is not, I repeat, *not* pronounced "MawREESE!" Also, technically Mauricetown is not within the Pinelands, but the Maurice River, designated as a National Scenic and Recreational River, makes up part of the Pinelands National Reserve border in this southern area of New Jersey, so it deserves mention. Look for directional signs from Route 47, which is part of the southern route of the New Jersey Pine Barrens Scenic Byway.

Mauricetown may be one of the most picturesque little villages in the Pinelands, if not the entire state, with "little" being the key word. A real sense of community can be sensed here. Located within Commercial Township in Cumberland County, it's composed of nine streets, six of which are fewer than 150 yards long, most of which are home to architecturally stunning houses. Most of the buildings have been beautifully restored; the majority are private residences. Architectural styles such as Italianate, Gothic Revival, Victorian and others can be seen; tours can be arranged via the Mauricetown Historical Society. Be sure to take a close look at the Methodist Church and its Mariners' Memorial Window. It was dedicated by the last surviving sea captain, Alonzo T. Bacon, and is inscribed with the names of sea captains and mates of sailing vessels lost between 1856 and 1914. The church's distinctive steeple was once used as a landmark for seamen. A drive—or, better yet, a stroll—through this village is like a trip back in time.

INSIDER'S TIP: Each February, Mauricetown Fire Hall hosts the Cumberland County Winter Eagle Festival, a day full of activities, walks, exhibits, speakers, book signings, vendors and tasty Down Jersey food. Birding enthusiasts young and old will not be disappointed as experts and volunteers from New Jersey Audubon/ Cape May Bird Observatory and Citizens United to Protect the Maurice River will be on hand with spotting scopes and a wealth of information to help identify wildlife and guide tours at various viewing sites. There is an admission fee, but if you enjoy birds and the outdoors, it's well worth it.

Mauricetown is a quaint riverfront village in the southern Pinelands. This beautiful building is the home of the Mauricetown Historical Society.

Just a few miles outside of Mauricetown is one of the few industries other than agriculture and fishing in this area, in the form of a large sand quarry. Dotting the landscape in this area are several large, deep pits from where the sand is harvested and then processed by a division of U.S. Silica Company. The sand here is reported to be 99 percent pure silica and is used for both industrial and recreational use. The old quarries eventually fill with water, and the result is ponds looking quite like the blue-green waters of the tropics. These ponds, however, are fenced off with No Trespassing/Swimming signs at regular intervals, so as tempting as they may look on a hot summer day, please don't go near them.

Just outside town, back on Route 47, is a startlingly modern diner called, appropriately enough, the Maurice River Diner. I'm told the food here is good, portions are generous and prices are reasonable. You're in "Down Jersey" now, so restaurants are scarce as farmland is plentiful. The Maurice River Diner is a good choice, especially if you have young ones in tow.

CHAPTER 17

Belleplain State Forest and Woodbine

BELLEPLAIN STATE FOREST

As you drive in this laid-back southern region, it will seem like "all roads lead to Belleplain." That's not far from the truth, partly because of its size and partly because of its fragmentation, as there are many privately owned properties interspersed within the state forest perimeters. Like much of the southern Pinelands, Belleplain is a great blend of pine/oak forest with lots of wetlands fringed by the characteristic Atlantic white cedars. This forest is a favorite stopover for migrating birds; in fact, thousands of birders flock to Belleplain each spring and fall to catch a glimpse of one of many feathered visitors. Beyond its lure for birders and bird photographers, this forest offers so much to its visitors, including extensive campgrounds near Lake Nummy, a twenty-six-acre lake named for the last chief of the Unalachtigo tribe of Native Americans, a branch of the Lenni-Lenape. Once a working cranberry bog, this pretty lake has a sandy beach for summertime swimming, paddle boating and fishing. A concession stand on site provides light food and canoe rentals. Campsites include spots for tents or recreational vehicles; lean-tos with propane heaters that sleep up to six; and yurts, which are round tents built on a wood frame that sleep up to five. All are available for a small fee year-round. Restrooms, showers and drinking water are available within walking distance. A special plus is the East Creek Cabin, which accommodates up to thirty people. It has a full kitchen and living room with fireplace. Its location on the lake and near hiking trails makes this is a wonderful place for scouting or other community getaways.

The visitors' center, staffed by friendly and efficient employees, is just inside the forest's main entrance off Route 550, although access to Belleplain can be had via a number of roadways surrounding its 21,320 acres. Stop in for a map and updates on events. A small per-car fee is charged between Memorial Day and Labor Day.

Woodbine

Woodbine is on the eastern outskirts of the state-owned Belleplain Forest, and this town has a very interesting history. It was founded in 1891 by Eastern European Jews who immigrated to this country to escape the violent Czarist mob riots, or pogroms, against them. Millionaire railroad tycoon and philanthropist Baron DeHirsch set up a fund that allowed the purchase of 5,300 acres in Dennis Township in Cape May. Immigrants from Poland and Russia were invited to settle this land as a community and, within a few years, had built a town and farms that eventually gave Woodbine a reputation as a model agricultural community. Incorporated as a borough of New Jersey in 1903, Woodbine became the first self-governed Jewish community.

The Sam Azeez Museum of Woodbine Heritage celebrates Jewish heritage and culture.

Today, the Brotherhood Synagogue, located on Washington Avenue, is home to the Sam Azeez Museum of Woodbine Heritage. This building, listed on the National Register of Historic Places, was built by its members and consecrated in 1896 and is still used for special worship services. The museum displays historic photographs, personal accounts and other artifacts, many of which have been donated by Woodbine residents. It's open to the public, and admission is free. The museum's mission statement is focused on hate and prejudice reduction, so this is a wonderful place to bring children of all races and religions for an education on diversity.

Woodbine's population is under three thousand today. It is home to one of only three airports in Cape May County and to many equestrian facilities that dot the landscape surrounding the town.

Chapter 18

Tuckahoe and Corbin City

Tuckahoe and Corbin City, located on either side of the Tuckahoe River, have a history dating back to pre-colonial times when the Native American Lenni-Lenape tribes favored this area as a prime fishing region. The name "Tuckahoe" is actually a Native American term for the fungus-like growth found at the base of trees that they used in bread making. Homage to its previous inhabitants can be seen throughout this area, a testament to the caring people who call this part of the Pinelands their home. Even the popular Tuckahoe Inn, an excellent upscale but casual restaurant on the banks of the river a bit east of town, has as its logo a silhouette of the head of a Native American. The inn serves the old-time Philadelphia-area classic meal of fried oysters and chicken salad. This restaurant is a popular gathering spot, especially in summer, when the Back Bay Café draws visitors from near and far. Its location on the Tuckahoe Bay is actually called Beesley's Point; during the summer, boaters can tie up at the dock to enjoy a meal here.

The Tuckahoe area was settled by Europeans in the late 1600s. Because of its proximity to the Atlantic via the Tuckahoe River and Egg Harbor Bay, industry flourished here, as in many coastal towns. Tuckahoe is a good example of an 1800s rural river town, as it was centered on maritime industries. Ships, especially two- and three-masted schooners, were built here and launched into the river. Bog iron and glassmaking were both important industries, as attested to by the nearby Aetna Furnace and Estell Glassworks. Because of the transportation offered via the river, railroads didn't come into the Tuckahoe area until the late 1800s, but once they did, Tuckahoe became a thriving railroad town. Dozens of trains heading to and from the shore towns of Atlantic City, Ocean City and Cape May passed through Tuckahoe daily.

Lester G. MacNamara Wildlife Management Area

Driving east on Tuckahoe Road, look for the big brown sign on the right with the words Tuckahoe Fish and Wildlife Management Area, Purchased in 1933 with Funds from the Sale of Hunting and Fishing Licenses, although the word "Tuckahoe" is almost invisible. The 34,231 total acres of this oldest wildlife management area in the state, renamed to honor the 1960s director of the New Jersey Fish and Game Council (which oversees the New Jersey Division of Fish and Wildlife), are considered an Important Birding Area (IBA) by the New Jersey Audubon Society for its variety of habitats, including tidal salt marsh, mixed upland forest and freshwater rivers and impoundments, which draw many birds. You'll find more than just birds here, however. A warm, sunny day may find a turtle napping on an emerged log or fisherman putting in his boat for a day on the Tuckahoe, Great Egg or Middle Rivers. There is a paved road at the sign that will take you through a very scenic oak pine and cedar forest, with a number of wetland areas adjacent to the road.

Cape May Seashore Lines

In an effort to recapture some of the romance of the days of railroad transportation, Cape May Seashore Lines was established. It currently offers two excursion services. One is a twelve-mile round trip between Rio Grande and Cape May City, and within the Pinelands is a thirty-mile round trip between Richland and Tuckahoe. Both operations are on the former Reading Company's steel speedway to the shore. Call or visit the website, as trips are seasonal.

Chapter 19

Estell Manor County Park

As you travel north on Route 50 toward Mays Landing, you will come across a gem of a park run by Atlantic County. Estell Manor was originally owned by the Estell family and was the site of Estellville Glassworks from 1825 to 1877. It was most likely the first glassworks that was able to produce both glass bottles and window glass. The Estell family owned and operated the factory until 1858, after which the factory had many owners. It finally closed completely, as did most other glassworks in the Pinelands, in 1877. The remains of the melting furnace, the pot house and the flattening house are still partially standing, and descriptive signage helps to envision the original buildings.

During World War I, Estell Manor became the location of a munitions plant called Bethlehem Loading Company. The area selected was a tract of land stretching from below Mays Landing to Petersburg, consisting mostly of swampy land, totaling approximately ten thousand acres. Railroads were built soon after groundbreaking to bring in necessary construction materials. The plant contained twenty-four miles of railroad track, administration buildings, cafeterias, change houses, police buildings and military barracks to house 1,100 soldiers who guarded the plant. This was followed by building a town, named Belcoville, to house thousands of employees. It included a school, bank, bowling alley and several stores. Today, some remains of the plant and administration buildings can be found within Estell Manor County Park. Outside of the park, concrete foundations and rail beds are all that remain of the town.

Estell Manor County Park in Atlantic County is the home of the former glassworks of the same name. The remains of the buildings, such as this melting furnace, are on display in the park, with descriptive signs in front of each.

Estell Manor County Park isn't just for history, however. A number of trails run through the park, and a 1.5-mile trail with exercise stations runs inside the paved loop road. You'll also find picnic areas, sport fields, fishing, boating and camping here.

For those interested in orienteering, map and compass courses are permanently installed at Estell Manor for the beginner, intermediate or expert. Instruction and loaner compasses are included in a four-hour session offered at no charge to the general public once a month, November through April.

The Warren E. Fox Nature Center located here is the Atlantic County Park System headquarters and holds a number of environmental education and recreation programs. Stop in here to pick up brochures and to view the environmental and live animal displays. You can also borrow bikes, helmets, softball equipment, volleyballs, horseshoes and soccer balls, all at no charge.

INSIDER'S TIP: Hungry for seafood? Just north of Estell Manor is a little red building on the east side of Route 50 called simply "Crabby's." As the sign says, it serves "Seafood and Suds," but don't let appearances deceive you. This small, *very* casual place (brown kraft paper and a roll of paper towels are laid out in front of you when you order) serves up some of the best seafood around; in fact, it's been the recipient of a number of awards from regional newspapers and food critics for its fantastic seafood, which includes blue claw crabs, Alaskan king, southern king and snow crab clusters, shrimp, scallops, clams and mussels. The she-crab soup gets rave reviews, as do the clams casino. Are you hungry yet? All-you-can-eat nights are popular, whether blue claw crabs, snow crab claws or shrimp, but the combo platters are huge as well. The prices are not bargain basement, and some items are market price so you have to ask, but if you want fresh seafood and don't mind getting a little dirty, this is the place to go.

Chapter 20

Mays Landing, Weymouth and Richland

Mays Landing

Historic Mays Landing Village, as so many areas here in the Pinelands, was once inhabited by Native Americans, specifically the Unalachtigo branch of the Lenni-Lenape tribe. It was first settled in 1695. Although it is believed that it was Peter Steelman who first settled here, this picturesque village was named for a Captain George May, who sailed up the Great Egg Harbor River on behalf of the London Company and established a shipyard and trading post here. Mays Landing soon became the center of shipbuilding in Atlantic County. Today, it serves as the county seat and is part of the Township of Hamilton. A bronze statue of a Lenni-Lenape Indian chief dedicated in 1981 stands in front of the courthouse, which was built in 1838 and is still in use today.

The river is an important part of Mays Landing, as can be seen by the many homes fringing its edges. The historic Inn at Sugar Hill, a small but highly rated bed-and-breakfast, is situated on the banks of the river and is a stunning sight as one enters Mays Landing via Route 50. This handsome building was built in 1846 by William Moore, manager of the Weymouth Furnace. After his death in 1876, the Moore Villa was home to several generations of the Abbotts, a prominent Mays Landing family, and was opened as a bed-and-breakfast by its current owner in 1987. The innkeeper's personal sailboat, *Grace*, is tied up at the dock of the inn, where outdoor dining is featured in season.

The Great Egg Harbor River was designated by the National Park Service as a National Wild and Scenic River in 1992. This photo taken in Mays Landing shows the historic Inn at Sugar Hill on the far shore.

On the western side of Lake Lenape is a two-thousand-acre park run by Atlantic County; the eastern side is home to Lenape Park, which is run by the township and is the location of the infamous Lake Lenape Lighthouse. The following excerpt from the July 1999 issue of *Lighthouse Digest Magazine* provides the history:

> *The Lake Lenape Lighthouse in Mays Landing, New Jersey was never a real lighthouse in the sense of the word, but it truly is a part of New Jersey's rich and interesting history as well as a popular landmark of the area.*
>
> *It was back in 1939 when the Leiling family, who owned the Lenape Park, commissioned Herman Dehn Sr. to build a lighthouse on the lake. First Dehn had to create an island for the lighthouse to be built on. He did this by using bags of mixed concrete and 30-gallon size drums to form the island's foundation. In the winter time he piled dirt onto the ice which would sink to the bottom in the spring thaw.*

The "singing tower" on the shores of Lake Lenape in Mays Landing is a popular landmark. It is best seen from Lake Lenape County Park across the lake, a popular boating spot.

Once the island was completed he built the 65-foot wooden tower with mostly simple hand tools and the help of some neighborhood children. The lighthouse with its five floors, connected with a semi-spiral staircase took four years to complete.

For many years the tower was known as the "singing tower" because of the hymns that were played from speakers that were installed atop the tower. When new owners, Ed & Winnie Young, took over the park in 1960's, local public officials said there were too many complaints from neighbors about the music and it had to stop. The children of the Youngs then took over the lighthouse, spending the nights there in the summer months.

Today, the lighthouse serves mainly as a storage building for beach and boating supplies, but is still a popular spot for those in love. Because of its romantic setting, many people have been married at the lighthouse.

The old lighthouse is an ongoing financial strain for the owners, who say they are constantly having to repair something at the lighthouse and have been for 15 years. But they haven't altered it and as Mr. Young once said, "We want to keep the nostalgia of the place and the lighthouse is a big part of that."

WEYMOUTH

Another of the Pinelands' "lost towns" is located on Route 559, just north of Route 322. This Atlantic County park is the site of an iron furnace and paper mill right along the Egg Harbor River. During its peak in the 1850s, this area included a furnace, a forge, a gristmill, a sawmill, the owner's mansion, a blacksmith's shop, a wheelwright, twenty workers' houses and a Methodist church.

Built in the 1800s, the furnace began iron production in 1801 and remained in production for about sixty years, making primarily cast-iron water pipes, along with some pots, stoves and nails. During the War of 1812, Weymouth Furnace supplied shot and bombs to the United States government, but as with other furnaces in and around the New Jersey Pinelands, by the 1860s,

Located along the Great Egg Harbor River north of Cape May, the tall smokestack of the Atlantic Paper Mill still stands in Weymouth County Park. This mill and the Weymouth Paper Mill produced paper from the 1860s until 1897.

it could no longer compete with the anthracite coal–powered furnaces being so much more affordably produced in Pennsylvania, and it went out of fire. Weymouth was also the site of two paper mills: Atlantic Paper Mills and Weymouth Paper Mills, both of which produced paper until the late 1800s.

Today, all that is left are the photographic remains of the paper mill and the large chimney stack, but this pretty park is a popular spot to begin canoe or kayak trips down the Great Egg Harbor River, which, like the Maurice River, has been designated as a National Wild and Scenic River by the National Park Service.

INSIDER'S TIP: A very nice restaurant and pub in Richland is the Rail Bar and Grill on Route 40. Its owner has renovated the restaurant and is taking great strides in bringing guests a "feels like home" experience—and it works! A brief stop here resulted in friendly conversation and some delicious buffalo wings.

RICHLAND

Traveling west on Route 40 will take you to Buena Vista Township (pronounced Byoona, not Bwena). Richland has the distinction of being home to Dalponte Farm, one of the largest mint farms in the country. In fact, in 2004, rum maker Bacardi paid Richland $5,000 to change its name to "Mojito" for two weeks in May in honor of the rum drink made with mint. A sign proclaiming WELCOME TO MOJITO stood on the side of Route 40 for two weeks. The following year, the owners of Dalponte Farms had a crop circle in the shape of the Bacardi bat carved into a six-acre swath of their mint fields in Buena Vista. Bacardi paid for the work, which took more than three hundred man hours. Bacardi purchases most of its mint from Dalponte Farms.

Richland Village, right along Route 40, is a railroad-themed area, with a train station for the Cape May Seashore Line. The village also has an old-fashioned general store, a restaurant, the Patcong Valley Model Railroad and other shops. A bit farther west along Route 40 will lead to the borough of Buena. To visit a nice local winery, follow the signs to Bellview Winery, located on Atlantic Street. Otherwise, take Route 690 north to Route 54, which leads to Hammonton, blueberry capital of the world.

Chapter 21

Hammonton

Continuing north on Route 54, keep a lookout for the endless fields of blueberry bushes as you near the Atlantic City Expressway—you'll know you've arrived in Hammonton, the "blueberry capital of the world." Route 54 (also named Twelfth Street) becomes Bellevue Avenue. This lovely street is filled with beautiful homes with varied architecture: Tudor, French Tudor, Victorian, Bungalow, Colonial Revival, Italianate and other styles line the streets just north of the business district. In the summer, green lawns are flanked with a rainbow of flowers. If you have time, another lovely street is Central Avenue.

Hammonton officially became a town in 1866. At that time, strawberries and sweet potatoes were its biggest crops; blueberries weren't even grown here until many years later. The mid-nineteenth century saw a large influx of Italian immigrants, and today Hammonton is second only to Providence, Rhode Island, in its percentage of residents proudly bearing Italian ancestry. In fact, a large bust of Christopher Columbus was dedicated in 1992, commemorating the 500th anniversary of his discovery of the New World.

Today, Hammonton's blueberry logo can be seen even on the water tower. Huge commercial blueberry farms can be seen just south of town. The berries grown here are what make New Jersey rank consistently in the top five states in the country for blueberry production.

The bust of Christopher Columbus was erected at Columbus Plaza in Hammonton, New Jersey, to commemorate the 500th anniversary of his discovery of America. The plaque reads, "Christopher Columbus: Man of History, Man of Courage, Man of Faith" and depicts the *Nina*, *Pinta* and *Santa Maria*. The statue was built through the efforts of nineteen various organizations in Hammonton, which celebrates its strong Italian heritage.

Blueberries run through an automated sorter that kicks out green or rotten berries and readies them for packaging.

INSIDER'S TIP: Looking for a place to pick your own blueberries while you're in blueberry country? Try B&B Farms at 250 South Mannheim Avenue in Egg Harbor City. It's my personal favorite because it's a quiet, family-run farm, and the bushes are loaded with berries. Berries are usually available between June 15 and August 1, but call Carolyn first to be sure. If you're traveling in the cold of winter, don't worry, you can still get Jersey blueberries. Of course, they'll be frozen and you might need to buy a case, but they taste great in pancakes and muffins, and there's nothing quite like homemade blueberry jam. Visit Blueberry Bill Farm just off the Atlantic City Expressway and Route 54, a few miles south of town. Just call Bill first to let him know you're coming.

Feast of Our Lady of Mount Carmel

Hammonton is home to the longest-running Italian festival in the United States, the Feast of Our Lady of Mount Carmel. Since its beginning in 1875 as a way for Italian immigrants to give thanks for their safe passage to America, it has grown to a six-day event with processions, music, carnival rides and, of course, authentic Italian food. The festival has a following made up of people who make an annual pilgrimage here as an act of faith, but most come for the fun and festivities.

Eagle Theatre

The Eagle Theatre was built in 1914 and was one of the first theaters to show silent movies. It closed in 1927 and fell to disrepair, but several years ago, thanks to hardworking volunteers and generous donations, it was authentically restored through private donations. Today, it is the premier center for movies and the arts in the region.

The Eagle Theatre in Hammonton was originally constructed in 1914 as a silent movie theater. It saw a variety of uses over the years, including as a church and storage facility. In 2007, in disrepair and on the verge of being demolished, the theater was purchased by the Hammonton Revitalization Corporation and restored to today's glory as a playhouse.

The Art Centers

Just around the corner from the Eagle Theatre is the Noyes Museum of Art's Satellite Gallery. Local artists' and artisans' works are showcased here on a rotating basis. The Hammonton Art Center, located just a block away on Bellevue Avenue, displays the artwork of regional artists and offers a variety of special events. Much of the artwork at both places depicts local animals, flowers, rivers and oceans. It's amazing to see the variety of excellent artwork that comes out of South Jersey. While strolling on Bellevue Avenue, be sure to stop into one of the several antique shops for a nostalgic look back at days of old.

The Wineries

Blueberries, arts and antiques aren't Hammonton's only claim to fame. With its location on the southern coastal plain of New Jersey, the climate in the region is similar to that of the coast of France, which of course is world famous for its top-quality wines, so the result is a superior quality grape. Here in the Pinelands of New Jersey, the wineries have garnered a huge amount of respect for their high-quality wines; several wineries have won gold medals as far away as San Francisco. The Hammonton area boasts several excellent wineries: Sharrott, DiMatteo, Valenzano, Plagido, Tomasello and Renault, among others. All offer tastings on weekends, and many are open during the week as well. Wine festivals take place at individual wineries, and most take part in "wine trail weekends," always popular events that draw locals and visitors alike.

For your own mini wine-tasting tour, I suggest starting at Sharrott Winery and then heading to Plagido, Tomasello and finally DiMatteo (call ahead for hours, especially during the week). These wineries are all within short driving

Wineries have become increasingly popular in the Pinelands as more and more people are learning of the quality of wine being produced. Here, owners of Sharrott Winery offer their wines for tasting to a group of guests.

distance of Hammonton, which has a good array of Italian restaurants with good food; most carry the local varieties. One of these is Annata Wine Bar, located on Bellevue Avenue just a block north of the train station. Over 160 wines from around the world are offered, as well as the regional wines, all in an upscale atmosphere. Food is consistently very good here; it's one of my favorite stops when I'm in Hammonton.

If you're thinking of making it a weekend, a Howard Johnson Inn is located on Route 30 right in Hammonton, and rates are quite reasonable. Of course, heading east on Route 30, also locally known as the White Horse Pike, for about thirty miles will take you to all the glitz and glamour of Atlantic City's casinos and resorts. Although not within the Pinelands National Reserve for obvious reasons, the wide boardwalk and clean white beaches of Atlantic City are world famous, and typical casino-style five-star dining and lodging are offered here. It is also home to the Atlantic City Aquarium with over one hundred varieties of sea creatures and a touch tank for the children; dolphin-watching cruises are also available. The 150-year-old Absecon Lighthouse, the third largest in the country, is situated in the northern part of Atlantic City. It's about a half hour drive east on Route 30, so easy to get to and a fun place for families. The kids will love climbing the 228 steps to the top for the spectacular view. It's certainly worth the small admission fee.

Insider's Tip: One of my favorite restaurant stops in Hammonton is Rocco's Town House, a local tavern/restaurant just a block west of Bellevue Avenue/Route 54 on Third Street. This hidden gem has been open since 1949, and the friendly staff here makes you feel right at home, just like most of the restaurants in the Pinelands. The décor hasn't changed much over the years, but it's all part of its charm. Rocco's offers a huge selection of craft beers, but go for the food. On Fridays between 4:00 p.m. and 6:00 p.m., the owner serves his own homemade pizza, compliments of the house. The crust is tender, and the ingredients taste right-off-the-farm fresh, nothing like commercial pizza pies. Rocco's is not to be missed if you're in town.

CHAPTER 22

Wheaton Arts and Cultural Center

Wheaton Village in Millville, Cumberland County, is located outside of the New Jersey Pinelands protection area but is still within the ecological Pine Barrens and is an important part of South Jersey's history. Glassmaking was a vital part of New Jersey's heritage, and here young and old alike can learn how it's made, as well as discover various educational and interesting interpretive programs and displays. The center is home to the Museum of American Glass, the Creative Glass Center of America International Fellowship Program, the Folklife Center (the largest in the state), a hot glass studio, several traditional craft studios, five museum stores, an event center and a picnic grove. The shops are open to the public, but there is an admission fee charged for the other attractions.

MUSEUM OF AMERICAN GLASS

Imagine a collection of over fifteen thousand pieces of both decorative and household glass, most of which are on permanent display, from early American bottles, jars and paperweights dating back to 1739 to stunning works of artistic glass created by contemporary glass artists. This is what you'll find at this museum, the most comprehensive exhibit of American glass in the world. Special tours are offered for glass collectors, as well as students of all ages.

GLASS STUDIO

The Wheaton Arts Glass Studio is home to resident and international artists, studio assistants, interns and a number of students at various phases of their education in glassmaking. Here, you can watch contemporary glass being blown in a replica of the 1800s T.C. Wheaton glass house. For an additional fee, "make-your-own" experiences are offered (by appointment only) where, with assistance from the professionals, you can learn to create a paperweight, vase, bowl or other vessel.

DOWN JERSEY FOLKLIFE CENTER

South Jersey has its own diverse culture, represented by over thirty-five ethnic, religious and occupational communities. The Down Jersey Folklife Center presents this rich blend of backgrounds via displays and exhibits, music, dance, craft demonstrations, concerts and other performances representing traditional art and artists and the folklife of the region. Just a few of the many traditions are African American quilt making, Barnegat Bay sneakboxes, split-oak basketry, Jersey Devil tales, fox-hunting Pinelands style, Puerto Rican *jibaro* music, Greek and Bulgarian circle dances and Native American beadwork and pine needle baskets. The center also has an archive full of music and videos about South Jersey traditions, which are available for visitors to watch. Concert series and workshops are offered for the public, and a number of "ritual performances" are presented throughout the year.

MUSEUM STORES

The museum stores include a general store, a Brownstone Emporium, a Christmas shop, the Arthur Gorham Paperweight Shop and the Gallery of Fine Craft. Probably the most popular, at least for those with children, is the general store with its famous candy counter. It also stocks a number of locally made glass items, handcrafted ceramics, specialty foods, wooden canes and walking sticks and classic toys—the list is endless.

The Brownstone Emporium is a boutique featuring clothing and jewelry from local designers, as well as items by Fair Trade Federation artists from the world over. The Christmas shop is contained within and offers a pretty variety of American Studio Glass ornaments and decorations made at Wheaton's Glass Studio. The Paperweight Shop is a collector's dream, with weights from world-renowned artists. The gallery offers one-of-a-kind contemporary sculpture and fine arts in glass, ceramics, wood, textiles and mixed media. The 1,200-square-foot exhibit room displays works by both new and established artists. Sweets Suite is a bake shop café located at the entrance to Wheaton Arts, offering fresh sandwiches, organic hot dogs, cupcakes, cookies, brownies, muffins and scones, along with a variety of beverages.

Located on the Maurice River, Millville's Glasstown Center Arts District is a growing area offering a number of art studios and galleries, artists' residences and other creatively interesting businesses. Also located in the Arts District are retail outlet stores, restaurants, antique shops, arts and pottery school established by the local college and a seven-hundred-foot river walk along the "wild and scenic" Maurice River.

Millville also has a nice variety of eateries, from fast-food drive-ins to Irish pubs and Greek restaurants. If you're considering a night's stay in or near this historic area, about a dozen brand-name hotels are located between Millville and Vineland, located about five miles away.

Afterword

New Jersey is a state of surprises. Because of all its cities in the northeastern corridor, it has a reputation of being overcrowded, congested and filled with crime. Literally millions of people arrive at Newark Liberty International Airport each year; what they see as they arrive is nothing like the rest of our beautiful state. The northwest region of New Jersey has lakes and streams, rolling hills and even a 220-foot replica of the Washington Monument on our highest peak, High Point in the Kittatinny Mountains at 1,803 feet.

New Jersey's 130 miles of shoreline offers some of the most beautiful beaches in the country. From the wide sandy beaches of Cape May and Atlantic City to Long Beach Island, Point Pleasant Beach and north to Sandy Hook, with dozens of other beautiful locations in between, there are beaches and towns geared to every age group, from infants to senior adults. Homes along these beautiful beaches range from small shore bungalows to multimillion-dollar mansions whose owners' names are kept secret for the sake of privacy.

The Garden State is rightfully named, too. Of course, the blueberry and cranberry production from the Pine Barrens ranks around third nationally, but New Jersey was also the third largest producer of spinach and the fourth largest producer of peaches in 2010. Add to that another five major vegetable crops coming in with a ranking of tenth or higher, and it's pretty obvious that we have lots of farmland in spite of our diminutive size. Anyone who has tasted Jersey corn or tomatoes knows that there is none better in the country.

Then there's our seafood. New Jersey has strict environmental regulations, some of the most stringent in the country. As a result, our coastal waters are clean and clear, and we enjoy delicious fresh seafood year-round. With major commercial fishing ports such as Cape May, Barnegat Light, Point Pleasant and Atlantic City, we get fresh scallops, clams, tuna, flounder and close to one hundred other varieties of seafood.

But the Pinelands, the magical, mysterious New Jersey Pinelands, is perhaps the biggest gem of all. Over one million acres nestled between New York City and Philadelphia, in a state that comes in at forty-sixth in size with 7,418 square miles and the densest in population second only to the District of Columbia. From most places in the forest you won't hear more than the songs of the birds. Its inhabitants, so maligned for so many years, are proud to call themselves Pineys and will extend a hand to help a respectful visitor to this special place on earth. If you show respect to the land and all it stands for, you will find you've been bitten by more than our mosquitoes. You will find you've become addicted to the sights, smells, flowers, trees, plants and, perhaps most importantly, the people that call the New Jersey Pinelands home. Just remember: treat all those you meet as you would expect to be treated. This includes our people, our wildlife and our forests and shores.

After all, you *don't* want to aggravate the Jersey Devil!

Appendix

Allaire State Park
4625 Atlantic Avenue
Farmingdale, NJ 07727
732-919-3500 (Allaire Village)
732-938-2371 (Nature Interpretive Center)
732-938-5524 (Pine Creek Railroad)
www.state.nj.us/dep/parksandforests/parks/allaire.html

Annata Wine Bar
216 Bellevue Avenue (Route 54)
Hammonton, NJ 08037
609-704-9797
www.annatawinebar.com

Atsion Recreation Area
Wharton State Forest
744 Route 206
Atsion, NJ 08088
609-268-0444
www.batstovillage.org/atsion.htm

B&B Farms
250 South Manneheim Avenue
Egg Harbor City, NJ 08215
609-965-5558

Barnegat Historical Society/Heritage Village
575 East Bay Avenue
Barnegat, NJ 08005
609-698-5284
www.barnegathistoricalsociety.com

Barnegat Lighthouse State Park
208 Broadway
Barnegat Light, NJ 08006
609-494-2016
www.state.nj.us/dep/parksandforests/parks/barnlig.html

Bass River State Forest
762 Stage Road
Tuckerton, NJ 08087
609-296-1114
www.state.nj.us/dep/parksandforests/parks/bass.html

Batsto Historic Village
4110 Batsto Road
Batsto, NJ 08037
www.batstovillage.org

Belleplain State Forest
1 Henkinsifkin Road
Woodbine, NJ 08270
609-861-2404
www.nj.gov/dep/parksandforests/parks/belle.html

Blueberry Bill Farm
914 11th Street
Hammonton, NJ 08037
609-561-6665
www.blueberrybill.com

The Bog
Bill Smith, Owner
Warren Grove, NJ 08005
609-698-4385

Brendan T. Byrne State Forest
MM 1, Route 72 East
Woodland Township, NJ 08088
609-726-1191
www.state.nj.us/dep/parksandforests/parks/byrne.html

Cape May National Wildlife Refuge
24 Kimbles Beach Road
Cape May Court House, NJ 08210
609-463-0994
www.fws.gov/northeast/capemay

Cape May Seashore Lines
www.capemayseashorelines.org

Chatsworth Cranberry Festival
Route 563 at Route 532
Chatsworth, NJ 08019
www.cranfest.org

Chatsworth/Woodland Township Historical Society
3890 Route 532 (White Horse Inn)
Chatsworth, NJ 08019
609-726-1053
www.chatsworthnjhistory.org

Cloverdale Farm County Park
34 Cloverdale Road
Barnegat, NJ 08005
609-971-3085
www.co.ocean.nj.us/OCParks

Crabby's
1413 Route 50
Belcoville (Mays Landing), NJ 08330
609-625-2722

DiMatteo Vineyards
951 Eighth Street (turn into service road)
Hammonton, NJ 08037
609-704-1414 / 609-567-3909
www.dimatteowinery.net

Double Trouble State Park
Double Trouble Road and Pinewald-Keswick Road
Bayville, NJ 08721
732-341-4098
www.nj.gov/dep/parksandforests/parks/double.html

Doyle's Pour House
345 South Main Street (Route 9)
Barnegat, NJ 08005
609-660-8300

Eagle Theatre
208 Vine Street
Hammonton, NJ 08037
609-704-5012
www.theeagletheatre.com

Edwin B. Forsythe Wildlife Refuge/Barnegat Division
Observation Platform off Bayshore Drive
Barnegat, NJ 08005
Primary Refuge: 800 Great Creek Road
Oceanville, NJ 08231
609-652-1665
www.fws.gov/northeast/forsythe

Estell Manor County Park
109 Route 50
Mays Landing, NJ 08330
609-645-5960
www.aclink.org/PARKS/mainpages/estell.asp

Forest Resource Education Center
Don Connor Boulevard
Jackson, NJ 08527
732-928-2360
www.njforestrycenter.org

Forked River Mountain Coalition
PO Box 219
Forked River, NJ 08731
609-971-1635
www.frmc.org

Franklin Parker Preserve
c/o New Jersey Conservation Foundation
Woodland Township (Chatsworth), NJ
www.njconservation.org/franklinparkerpreserve.htm

Green Bank Inn
1301 Route 542
Green Bank, NJ 08215
609-965-5630

Hammonton Arts Center
219 Bellevue Avenue
Hammonton, NJ 08037
609-67-5360
hammontonartscenter.webs.com

Hammonton Historical Society
333 Vine Street
Hammonton, NJ 08037
609-270-7652
www.historicalsocietyofhammonton.org

Headley Farm Market
(Pine Bridge Branch, New Jersey Cranberries)
467 Route 9
West Creek, NJ 08092
609-618-6706

Howard Johnson Inn of Hammonton
308 South White Horse Pike (Route 30)
Hammonton, NJ 08037
609-561-5700
www.hojo.com

Inn at Sugar Hill
5704 Mays Landing–Somers Point Road
Mays Landing, NJ 08330
609-625-2226
www.innatsugarhill.com

Jacques Cousteau Coastal Center
130 Great Bay Boulevard
Tuckerton, NJ 08087
609-812-0649
www.jcnerr.org/tuckerton.html

Jakes Branch County Park
1100 Double Trouble Road
Beachwood, NJ 08722
732-281-2750

Lakehurst Historical Society
300 Center Street
Lakehurst, NJ 08733
732-657-8864
www.lakehurstnj.org/historicalmain.html

Lenape County Park
6303 Harding Highway
Mays Landing, NJ 08330
609-625 8219
www.aclink.org/PARKS/mainpages/Lake_Lenape.asp

Lighthouse Center for Natural Resource Education
Seventh Street and Navajo Drive
Waretown, NJ 08758
609-698-8003
www.experiencebarnegatbay.org

Lower Bank Tavern
1509 Route 542
Lower Bank, NJ 08215
609-965-6936
www.pineypower.com/lowerbanktavern.htm

Manahawkin Mart Shoppes/Flea Market
657 East Bay Avenue
Manahawkin, NJ 08050
609-597-1017
www.manahawkinfleamarket.com

Maurice River Diner
3830 Route 47
Port Elizabeth, NJ 08327
856-327-4433
www.themauriceriverdiner.com

Mauricetown Historical Society
1229 Front Street
Mauricetown, NJ
856-785-1137
www.mauricetownhistoricalsociety.org

Mill Rock Cranberry Farm
363 Pleasant Mills Road (Route 542)
Hammonton, NJ 08037
609-561-4705

Millville "Glasstown" Arts District
800-877-4957
www.glasstownartsdistrict.com

Motts Creek Inn
200 East Motts Creek Road
Galloway, NJ 08205
609-652-1555
www.mottscreekinn.net

Mud City Crab House
1185 East Bay Avenue
Manahawkin, NJ 08050
609-978-3660
www.mudcitycrabhouse.com

Navy Lakehurst Historical Society
PO Box 328
Lakehurst, NJ 08733
732-818-7520 (tour information)
www.nlhs.com

New Jersey Audubon/Cape May Bird Observatory
Center for Research and Education
600 Route 47 North
Cape May Court House, NJ 08210
609-861-0700
www.birdcapemay.org

New Jersey Coastal Heritage Trail
www.nps.gov/neje/index.htm

New Jersey Pinelands Commission
15 Springfield Road
New Lisbon, NJ 08064
609-894-7300
www.state.nj.us/pinelands

North Pemberton Railroad Station Museum, Rail Trail and Gift Shop
3 Fort Dix Road
Pemberton, NJ 08068
609-894-0546
www.pthtrust.org/history.htm

Noyes Gallery at Hammonton
5 Second Street
Hammonton, NJ 08037
609-561-8006
www.noyesmuseum.org/hammonton.html

Noyes Museum of Art
733 Lily Lake Road
Oceanville, NJ 08231
609-652-8848
www.noyesmuseum.org

Our Lady of Mount Carmel Feast
Mount Carmel Lane
Hammonton, NJ 08037
609-561-4818
www.mountcarmelsociety.homestead.com

Oyster Creek Inn
41 Oyster Creek Road
Leeds Point, NJ 08220
609-652-8565
www.oystercreekinnnj.com

Pic-a-Lilli Inn
866 Route 206
Shamong, NJ 08088
www.picalilli.com

Pinelands Preservation Alliance
17 Pemberton Road
Southampton, NJ 08088
609-859-8860
www.pinelandsalliance.org

Plagido's Winery
570 North First Road
Hammonton, NJ 08037
609-567-4633
www.plagidoswinery.com

Popcorn Park Zoo
Humane Way at Lacey Road
Forked River, NJ 08731
609-693-1900
www.ahscares.org

The Rail Bar and Grill
1252 Harding Highway (Route 40)
Richland, NJ 08350
856-697-RAIL
www.therailbarandgrill.net

Renault Winery
72 North Bremen Avenue
Egg Harbor City, NJ 08215
www.renaultwinery.com

Rova Farms
120 Cassville Road (Route 571)
Jackson, NJ 08527
732-928-0928
www.rovafarm-rcc.org

Sam Azeez Museum of Woodbine Heritage
610 Washington Avenue
Woodbine, NJ 08270
609-861-5355
www.thesam.org

Shamong Diner
7 Willow Grove Road
Shamong, NJ 08088
609-268-1182
www.shamongdiner.com

Sharrott Winery
370 South Egg Harbor Road (Route 561)
Blue Anchor, NJ 08037
609-567-9463
www.sharrottwinery.com

Smithville Historic Village
1 New York Road
Smithville, NJ 08205
609-652-7777
www.historicsmithvillenj.com

Spiaggia e Luna
696 East Bay Avenue
Barnegat, NJ 08005
609-660-2000
www.spiaggiaeluna.com

Stafford Township Historical Society
West Bay Avenue (across from Lake)
Manahawkin, NJ 08050
www.staffordhistory.org

St. Vladimir's Russian Orthodox Memorial Church
134 Perrineville Road
Jackson, NJ 08527
732-928-1248
www.stvladimirnj.org

Sweet Jenny's Restaurant at the Hurricane House
688 East Bay Avenue
Barnegat, NJ 08005
609-489-4203

Sweetwater Riverdeck
2780 Seventh Avenue
Sweetwater, NJ 08037
www.sweetwaterriverdeck.com

Tabernacle Township
163 Carranza Road
Tabernacle, NJ 08088
www.townshipoftabernacle-nj.gov

Tomasello Winery
255 North White Horse Pike (Route 30)
Hammonton, NJ 08037
609-561-0567
www.tomasellowinery.com

Tuckahoe Inn
1 Harbor Road
Beesley's Point, NJ 08223
609-390-3322
www.tuckahoeinn.com

Tuckerton Historical Society
35 Leitz Boulevard and Wisteria Lane
Little Egg Harbor, NJ 08087
609-294-1547
www.tuckertonhistoricalsociety.org

Tuckerton Seaport
120 West Main Street (Route 9)
Tuckerton, NJ 08087
609-296-8868

Valenzano Winery
1090 Route 206
Shamong, NJ 08088
609-268-6731
www.valenzanowine.com

Wells Mills County Park
905 Wells Mills Road (Route 532)
Waretown, NJ 08758
609-971-3085
www.co.ocean.nj.us/OCParks

Wheaton Arts and Cultural Center
1501 Glasstown Road
Millville, NJ 08332
800-998-4552
www.wheatonarts.org

Whitesbog Preservation Trust
120–34 Whitesbog Road
Browns Mills, NJ 08015
609-893-4646
www.whitesbog.org

Index

C

D

E

F

G

H

I

J

K

L

M

N

O

P

About the Author

Cathy Antener has had a fascination with the New Jersey Pinelands since moving to this area from Monmouth County, New Jersey, in the late 1970s. A career in the Ocean County Parks and Recreation Department enhanced her knowledge, and in 1998, she created PineyPower.com, a website covering just about everything about New Jersey's Pinelands. With its extensive information, photos and calendar of events, the website has grown to over 150 pages and has become a favorite for thousands of fans of the Pinelands across the country and even the world. Cathy has taken her knowledge to another level: for the past several years, she has offered guide services for bus companies and tour operators bringing visitors to the Pinelands area. She organizes and narrates full-day tours for groups from fifteen to fifty, sharing her knowledge of the area by offering narrated tours of the cranberry and blueberry harvests, Pine Barrens, wineries and Pinelands coastal areas. She also assists a local master basket weaver in teaching the ancient art of basketry to groups in the area.

Cathy frequently explores the million-acre Pinelands preservation area, where she might canoe, hike, visit museums or just enjoy the local restaurants and shops and chat with its colorful and friendly residents. Since

Ocean County contains so much Pinelands area, Cathy sits on the Board of Directors of the Southern Ocean County Chamber of Commerce, an active tourism-based organization of over five hundred members.

Cathy lives in the Pinelands of Barnegat, where her own naturalized property is the setting for many of her nature photographs, including plants, birds, insects and even an occasional endangered plant.